100 POETS

JOHN CAREY

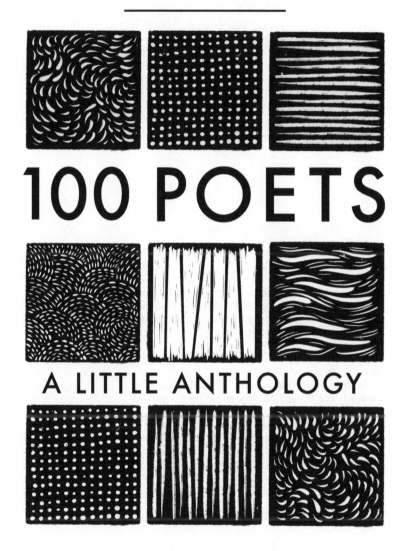

100 POETS

A LITTLE ANTHOLOGY

YALE UNIVERSITY PRESS
NEW HAVEN AND LONDON

For information about this and other Yale University Press publications, please contact:
U.S. Office: sales.press@yale.edu   yalebooks.com
Europe Office: sales@yaleup.co.uk   yalebooks.co.uk

Set in Minion Pro by IDSUK (DataConnection) Ltd
Printed in Great Britain by TJ Books, Padstow, Cornwall

Library of Congress Control Number: 2021940113

ISBN 978-0-300-25801-1

A catalogue record for this book is available from the British Library.

10 9 8 7 6 5 4 3 2 1

CONTENTS

INTRODUCTION

This book is a follow-up to *A Little History of Poetry* (2020). But it is also completely independent. Readers of it do not need to have read *A Little History*.

I have chosen 100 poets, mostly but not exclusively English and American, who seem to me outstanding. Some of them are represented here by a single work. With others, I offer a selection from the whole range of their poetic output.

Mostly the poets appear in chronological order. But sometimes, as in *A Little History*, I have abandoned strict chronology so as to draw attention to striking similarities or differences that span the centuries.

A poem seems a fragile thing. Change a word, and it is broken. But poems outlive empires and survive the devastation of conquests. I hope you will find poems in this book that remain with you for life.

INTRODUCTION

HOMER

Homer's two epics are the bedrock of European literature. No one knows who Homer was, exactly where he lived or whether the poems are by one poet or several. They are very different. The *Odyssey* is an adventure story, but the *Iliad* is the first war poem. It tells of the battles between Greeks and Trojans in the last few weeks of the siege of Troy, culminating in the defeat of the Trojans and the killing of the Trojan hero Hector by the Greek warrior Achilles.

Over the ages both epics have been translated into many languages. An early English translation was by Shakespeare's contemporary George Chapman. It was in this version that the poet John Keats, who knew no Greek, first read Homer, and he recalls his sense of awe-struck discovery in his sonnet 'On First Looking into Chapman's Homer' ('Much have I travelled in the realms of gold').

There is a famous scene in the *Iliad*, Book 6, where, during a pause in the fighting, Hector's wife Andromache tries to persuade him not to go back into the battle. He tells her he would be ashamed to behave in so cowardly a way. But his speech reveals that he knows Troy will fall, he will be killed, his little son will be fatherless and Andromache will be widowed – 'some rude Greek will lead thee weeping hence', as he foretells in Chapman's translation:

This said, he reacht to take his sonne, who (of his armes afraid,
And then the horse-haire plume, with which, he was so ouerlaid,
Nodded so horribly) he clingd, backe to his nurse, and cride.
Laughter affected his great Sire, who dost, and laid aside

His fearfull Helme; that on the earth, cast round about it, light;
Then tooke and kist his louing sonne; and (ballancing his weight
In dancing him) these louing vowes to liuing *ioue* he vsde,
And all the other bench of gods: O you that haue infusde
Soule to this Infant; now set downe, this blessing on his starre:
Let his renowne be cleare as mine, equall his strength in warre;
And make his reigne so strong in Troy, that yeares to come may
     yeeld
His facts this fame; (when rich in spoiles, he leaues the conquerd
     field
Sowne with his slaughters.) These high deeds, exceed his fathers
     worth:
And let this eccho'd praise supply, the comforts to come forth
Of his kind mother, with my life. This said; th'Heroicke Sire
Gaue him his mother; whose faire eyes, fresh streames of loues
     salt fire,
Billow'd on her soft cheekes, to heare, the last of *Hector*s speech;
In which his vowes comprisde the summe, of all he did beseech
In her wisht comfort. So she tooke, into her odorous brest,
Her husband's gift; who (mou'd to see, her heart so much
     oppresst)
He dried her teares; and thus desir'd: Afflict me not (deare wife)
With these vaine griefes; He doth not liue, that can disioyne my life
And this firme bosome; but my Fate; and Fate, whose wings can
     flie?
Noble, ignoble, Fate controuls: once borne, the best must die.

Hector's nobility would be out of place in the *Odyssey*, where the interest lies in the ordeals that wily Odysseus manages to survive. Some of them have become legendary, including Scylla and Charybdis, a man-eating female monster and a whirlpool, also female, that Odysseus and his mariners have to steer between. The following passages are from Emily Wilson's 2017 translation.

In the *Odyssey*, Book 12, the enchantress Circe forewarns Odysseus of the twin danger. There is a rock, she recounts:

> . . . and on it
> there grows a fig tree with thick leaves. Beneath,
> divine Charybdis sucks black water down.
> Three times a day she spurts it up; three times
> she glugs it down. Avoid that place when she
> is swallowing the water. No one could
> save you from death then, even great Poseidon.
> Row fast, and steer your ship alongside Scylla,
> since it is better if you lose six men
> than all of them.

Circe does not conceal how fearsome Scylla is:

> She has twelve dangling legs and six long necks
> with a gruesome head on each, and in each face
> three rows of crowded teeth, pregnant with death.
> Her belly slumps within the hollow cave;
> she keeps her heads above the yawning chasm
> and scopes around the rock, and hunts for fish.
> She catches dolphins, seals, and sometimes even
> enormous whales . . .

Just as Circe predicts, Scylla snatches six of Odysseus's men:

> But while our frightened gaze was on Charybdis,
> Scylla snatched six men from the ship – my strongest,
> best fighters. Looking back from down below,
> I saw their feet and hands up high, as they
> were carried off. In agony they cried
> to me and called my name – their final words.
> As when a fisherman out on a cliff
> casts his long rod and line set round with oxhorn
> to trick the little fishes with his bait;
> when one is caught, he flings it gasping back
> onto the shore – so these men gasped as Scylla
> lifted them up high to her rocky cave

and at the entrance ate them up – still screaming,
still reaching out to me in their death throes.
That was the most heartrending sight I saw
in all the time I suffered on the sea.

At the end of the *Odyssey*, Odysseus returns to Ithaca in disguise and slaughters the suitors who have been pestering his wife, Penelope. The handmaidens who have betrayed Penelope and consorted with the suitors are executed, in what is the first description of a hanging in literature and the last of the poem's horrors. Telemachus, Odysseus's son, decrees their doom and organises the executioners:

... 'I refuse to grant these girls
a clean death, since they poured down shame on me
and Mother, when they lay beside the suitors'.

At that, he wound a piece of sailor's rope
round the rotunda and round the mighty pillar,
stretched up so high no foot could touch the ground.
As doves or thrushes spread their wings to fly
home to their nests, but someone sets a trap –
they crash into a net, a bitter bedtime;
just so the girls, their heads all in a row,
were strung up with the noose around their necks
to make their death an agony. They gasped,
feet twitching for a while, but not for long.

SAPPHO
(c.630–c.570 BC)

Almost nothing is known of Sappho's life. She was born into a wealthy family on the island of Lesbos, and almost all her poetry has been lost. Only about 650 lines survive, mostly consisting of fragments. Her poetry was hugely admired in antiquity, and she seems to have been regarded as the equal of Homer. She was called 'The Poetess', and Homer 'The Poet'.

Her work is much closer to our modern idea of poetry than Homer's. She wrote short lyrics, not epics, and her subject was love, not war or adventure. A poem known only as 'Fragment 31' is the first description of passionate love by a woman in Western literature. It describes her shock when she sees her lover talking and laughing with a man. The complex of emotions it expresses is cited as an example of sublimity in *On the Sublime*, the first surviving literary critical treatise, written in Greek in the first century AD.

This translation is by Mary Barnard.

FRAGMENT 31

He is more than a hero

He is a god in my eyes –
the man who is allowed
to sit beside you – he

who listens intimately
to the sweet murmur of
your voice, the enticing

laughter that makes my own
heart beat fast. If I meet
you suddenly, I can't

speak – my tongue is broken;
a thin flame runs under
my skin; seeing nothing,

hearing only my own ears
drumming, I drip with sweat;
trembling shakes my body

and I turn paler than
dry grass. At such times
death isn't far from me.

VIRGIL
(70 BC– 19 BC)

The first English translation of Virgil's *Aeneid* was by Henry Howard, Earl of Surrey, around 1540. He is particularly good at sinister effects and tragic ironies. In Book 2 Aeneas, having reached Carthage, tells Dido of the fall of Troy. The game-changer, he recounts, was the wooden horse. The Greeks left this enormous model, higher than Troy's walls, apparently as a gift to the Trojans, and then sailed away. The Trojans rejoiced. Only the priest, Laocoön, suspected a trick, uttering one of the most famous sentences in literature: *Timeo Danaos et dona ferentes*, which Surrey translates: 'I dread the Greeks – yea, when they offer gifts!' Laocoön throws a spear at the horse:

> Which tremling stack, and shoke within the side,
> Wherwith the caues gan hollowly resound.

This proof of the horse's hollowness should be enough to alert the Trojans. But, before they can react, two vast serpents appear out at sea:

> Which plied towardes the shore – I lothe to tell –
> With rered brest lift vp aboue the seas;
> Whose bloody crestes aloft the waues were seen.
> The hinder part swame hidden in the flood;
> Their grisly backes were linked manifold.
> With sound of broken waues they gate the strand,
> With gloing eyen, tainted with blood and fire;

Whose waltring tongs did lick their hissing mouthes.
We fled away . . .

The serpents have been sent by Juno, who hates the Trojans, and they twist themselves round Laocoön and his two sons, crushing them to death. Their death struggles are depicted in one of the most famous statues to survive from antiquity, excavated in 1506 and now in Rome, but replicated all over the world.

The Trojans take the serpents to mean that Laocoön was wrong, and has offended the goddess, so they knock down part of Troy's walls and drag the horse inside:

In hope thereby the goddesse wrath tappease.
We cleft the walles and closures of the towne,
Whereto all helpe, and vnderset the feet
With sliding rolles, and bound his neck with ropes.
This fatall gin thus ouerclambe our walles,
Stuft with armed men; about the which there ran
Children and maides, that holly carolles sang;
And well were they whoes hands might touch the cordes.
With thretning chere thus slided through our town
The subtil tree, to Pallas temple ward.

'Gin' in line 5 means both 'engine' and 'snare'. The Trojans spend the day rejoicing and sleep tight when night falls, believing the war is over:

When, well in order comes the Grecian fleet
From Tenedon, toward the costes well knowne,
By frendly silence of the quiet moone.

The Greek warriors, Odysseus among them, slide down ropes from the horse and the slaughter begins. Aeneas, instructed by his mother, the goddess Venus, escapes, carrying his father, Anchises, and leading his little boy Ascanius, but his wife, Creusa, is lost in the carnage.

In Book 4 Virgil relates how Aeneas reaches Carthage, how he and Dido become lovers, how Jupiter sends Mercury to order Aeneas to leave Carthage – his destiny is to found Rome – and how Dido, mad with grief and rage, kills herself. She tricks her sister Anna into building a funeral pyre, on the pretence that if they fill it with things Aeneas has left behind and set light to it, it will magically free her from her love for him. Then she climbs the pyre, finds one of Aeneas's swords and stabs herself. But she cannot die until Juno sends Proserpina to cut her thread of life. Out at sea Aeneas sees the blaze of the funeral pyre.

Surrey's blank verse is a cumbersome medium for all this passion and melodrama, but John Conington's breathless, eight-syllable rhymed lines carry the poem convincingly to its operatic finale. Maddened by love and anger, Dido curses herself for not killing Aeneas when he was in her power, and killing Ascanius too, and feeding the son to the father in a ghastly imitation of the Thyestean banquet:

> O had I rent him limb from limb
> And cast him o'er the waves to swim,
> His friends, his own Ascanius killed,
> And with the child the father filled!
> Yet dangers in the strife had been: –
>   Who prates of danger here?
> A death-devoted, desperate queen,
>   What foe had I to fear?
> No, I had sown the flame broadcast,
> Had fired the fleet from keel to mast,
> Slain son and sire, stamped out the race,
> And thrown at length, with stedfast face
>   Myself upon the bier.

Virgil likens Dido to a Bacchante, one of the women who tore the singer Orpheus to pieces in a drunken frenzy. She is compared, too, to a stricken deer, unable to shake love's arrow from her body (an image that was to live on in the work of many poets). These associations, reducing her to a crazy female, contrast with Virgil's comparison of the dependably male Aeneas to an oak tree, buffeted by tempests yet standing firm.

Anna arrives, too late, to find her sister dying:

Her hands with slaughter sprinkled o'er,
And the fell weapon spouting gore.

She climbs the pyre and clasps her in a last embrace:

Enfolds her in her robe, and dries
The purple that her bosom dyes.
The dull eyes ope, as drowsed by sleep,
Then close: the death-wound gurgles deep.
Thrice on her arm she raised her head,
Thrice sank exhausted on the bed,
Stared with blank gaze aloft, around
For light, and groaned as light she found.

Then Juno sends Proserpina to cut her thread of life.

Dido did not recommend herself as a tragic heroine to Elizabethan dramatists, with the exception of Christopher Marlowe. His play *Dido, Queen of Carthage*, written in collaboration with Thomas Nashe, uses Surrey's translation, but also leaves some lines in the original Latin. It is the only Marlowe play with a woman as the central character, and Dido's vacillating passions carry little conviction. More recognisably Marlovian is Dido's wooer, Iarbas, who fantasises revenge when he hears that Dido and Aeneas have become lovers:

Nature, why mad'st me not some poysonous beast,
That with the sharpnes of my edged sting
I might haue stakte them both vnto the earth,
Whil'st they were sporting in this darksome Caue?

HORACE
(65 BC–8 BC)

Horace's best-known poems are his *Odes,* and these two are among the most famous. They are both from Book 3. In the first (3.13) he celebrates the deliciously cool fountain at his little farm in the countryside near Rome. He promises to sacrifice a young goat in honour of the fountain. We are made to feel the cruelty of the sacrifice, which adds seriousness to a light-hearted poem. He promises, too, to commemorate, in verse, the holly tree (ilex) that grows above the cavern from which the fountain flows – and the poem he is writing of course does that.

ODE 3.13

Bandusia's fount, in clearness crystalline,
O worthy of the wine, the flowers we vow!
Tomorrow shall be thine
A kid, whose crescent brow

Is sprouting all for love and victory.
In vain: his warm red blood, so early stirr'd.
Thy gelid stream shall dye,
Child of the wanton herd.

Thee the fierce Syrian star, to madness fired,
Forbears to touch: sweet cool thy waters yield

To ox with ploughing tired,
And lazy sheep afield.

Thou too one day shall win proud eminence
'Mid honour'd founts, while I the ilex sing
Crowning the cavern, whence
Thy babbling wavelets spring.

The second poem (3.26) is Horace's farewell to love, or sort of. He has, he boasts, done pretty well in that line. But he's getting old, and it's time to stop. So he will lay aside the equipment he has used on his amorous adventures. 'Links' (line 7) means torches carried by 'link boys' to light his way through the streets at night. Cyprus, and Memphis in Egypt (lines 9 and 10), were sacred to Venus. But the closing lines reveal that's there's life in the old dog yet, or anyway desire, and he asks Venus to punish Chloe for rejecting his advances.

ODE 3.26

For ladies' love I late was fit,
And good success my warfare blesst.
But now my arms, my lyre I quit,
And hang them up to rust or rest.

Here, where arising from the sea
Stands Venus, lay the load at last,
Links, crowbars, and artillery,
Threatening all doors that dared be fast.

O goddess! Cyprus owns thy sway,
And Memphis, far from Thracian snow;
Raise high thy lash, and deal me, pray,
That haughty Chloe just one blow!

Both translations are by John Conington, a professor of Latin at Oxford University, who successfully captures Horace's succinctness – no mean feat.

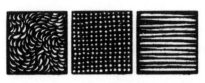

OVID
(43 BC–AD 17)

The first English translation of Ovid's *Metamorphoses* was by Arthur Golding. Published in 1567, it turns Ovid's lithe Latin into laborious 14-syllable lines, rhymed in couplets. This, however, was the translation Shakespeare had to make do with. Not until Ted Hughes's *Tales from Ovid* (1997) did an English version appear that could match Ovid in speed and suppleness. This is Hughes's version of the Salmacis and Hermaphroditus story from Book 4. Salmacis, a water nymph, falls in love with a beautiful human boy and secretly watches him undress and go for a swim:

> 'I've won!' shrieked Salmacis. 'He's mine!'
> She could not help herself.
> 'He's mine!' she laughed, and with a couple of bounds
> Hit the pool stark naked
> In a rocking crash and thump of water –
> The slips of her raiment settling wherever
> They happened to fall. Then out of the upheaval
> Her arms reach and wind round him,
> And slippery as the roots of big lilies
> But far stronger, her legs below wind round him.
> He flounders and goes under. All his strength
> Fighting to get back up through a cloud of bubbles
> Leaving him helpless to her burrowing kisses.
> Burning for air, he can do nothing

As her hands hunt over him, and as her body
Knots itself every way around him
Like a sinewy otter
Hunting some kind of fish
That flees hither and thither inside him,
And as she flings and locks her coils
Around him like a snake
Around the neck and legs and wings of an eagle
That is trying to fly off with it,
And like ivy which first binds the branches
In its meshes, then pulls the whole tree down,
And as the octopus –
A tangle of constrictors, nippled with suckers,
That drag towards a maw –
Embraces its prey.

But still Hermaphroditus kicks to be free
And will not surrender
Or yield her the least kindness
Of the pleasure she longs for,
And rages for, and pleads for
As she crushes her breasts and face against him
And clings to him as with every inch of her surface.
'It's no good struggling,' she hisses.
'You can strain, wrestle, squirm, but cannot
Ever get away from me now.
The gods are listening to me.
The gods have agreed we never, never
Shall be separated, you and me.'

The gods heard her frenzy – and smiled.

And there in the giddy boil the two bodies
Melted into a single body
Seamless as the water.

ANONYMOUS ANGLO-SAXON

The Battle of Maldon was fought on 11 August 991, beside the River Blackwater in Essex. A Viking force estimated at about 3,000 men had sailed up the river and landed on an island, connected to the mainland by a narrow causeway. Opposing the invasion was Byrhtnoth, an alderman of Essex, with a levy of local farmers and villagers. Three of his men guarded the causeway, preventing the Vikings from crossing, and the Viking chief asked Byrhtnoth to allow his warriors across so that they could fight on equal terms. Byrhtnoth consented, and in the ensuing fight he and his men were slaughtered.

This fragment from *The Battle of Maldon*, translated from the Anglo-Saxon by John Carey, describes the closing stage of the battle. The speech of Byrhtnoth's follower, Byrhtwold, one of the last to die, is among the most famous passages in Anglo-Saxon poetry.

The fighter Wistan is called both Thurstan's son and Wighelm's. Presumably Thurstan was his father and Wighelm his mother.

So shields were shattered   and the seamen surged
                      forward
Furious was the fight   spears transfixed
Broken bodies   Then brave Wistan
Thurstan's son   was the seamen's bane
Three of the throng   he thrust his spear through
Before Wighelm's bairn   bit the dust.
Stiff was the war play   warriors stood fast
Mired in massacre   men dropped dead

Went to their doom   wearied with wounds.
Then each of the brothers   Oswald and Eadwold
Rallied the ranks   roared at their kinsmen
To grapple with the foe   in the grim conflict
Wield their weapons   without weakness.
Then Byrhtwold spoke   brandished his shield
A sure-footed oldster   ash-spear aloft
Shouted defiance   above the war-din
'Hope shall be the higher   heart the keener
Mettle the more   as our might lessens.
Here lies our lord   all lopped and hewn
  Our mighty man mangled   Ever may he mourn
Who now from this warfare   weakly shrinks.
I am withered by age   and will not go from here.
By my dear lord   I desire to die
To lie by the side   of my loved leader.'

DANTE ALIGHIERI
(c.1265–1321)

Dante's *Divine Comedy* waited almost five centuries before anyone translated it into English, partly because its Catholic theology was objectionable to English Protestants. The first English translation was by the Irish cleric Henry Boyd in 1802, and does not seem to have received much notice. However, the next, by Henry Cary in 1814, attracted the attention of Byron, Scott, Keats, Shelley, Wordsworth and other British Romantics, because of the Paolo and Francesca episode, which they interpreted as a protest against despotic authority.

Francesca was the daughter of Guido da Polenta, lord of Ravenna, and in 1275 he married her to Giovanni Malatesta, Lord of Rimini, to seal a political alliance. While in Rimini she fell in love with Giovanni's younger brother, Paolo, and their secret relationship lasted some 10 years, until Giovanni surprised them in Francesca's bedroom and killed them both.

In the *Inferno*, Dante finds them in the second circle of hell, reserved for the lustful. They are swept about eternally and helplessly, like birds, by a whirling, lightless storm, because they allowed themselves to be swept about by their passions.

Keats's friend Leigh Hunt wrote a version of the Paolo and Francesca episode called *The Story of Rimini* (1816) while he was in prison for libelling the Prince Regent, and Keats wrote a sonnet about it. In Thomas Love Peacock's *Nightmare Abbey* (1818) Mr Listless notices that Dante has suddenly become fashionable among the romantically inclined and remarks, 'I am afraid I must read him some wet mornings'. Byron wrote his own verse translation of the episode, called *Francesca of Rimini*, which was published in 1820. It was inspired by his mistress, Countess Teresa Guiccioli, who, like Francesca, came from Ravenna, was trapped in a marriage of convenience and was unfaithful to her husband.

Byron, like Dante, uses terza rima, whereas Cary had used blank verse. In *Inferno* 5.73–143, Dante recognises Francesca and, at his request, she tells the story of her love and how it began:

> 'We read one day for pastime, seated nigh,
> Of Lancilot, how Love enchained him too.
> We were alone, quite unsuspiciously.
> But oft our eyes met, and our Cheeks in hue
> All o'er discoloured by that reading were;
> But one point only wholly us o'erthrew;
> When we read the long-sighed-for smile of her,
> To be thus kissed by such devoted lover,
> He, who from me can be divided ne'er,
> Kissed my mouth, trembling in the act all over;
> Accurséd was the book and he who wrote!
> That day no further leaf we did uncover.'
> While thus one Spirit told us of their lot,
> The other wept, so that with Pity's thralls
> I swooned, as if by Death I had been smote,
> And fell down even as a dead body falls.

GEOFFREY CHAUCER
(1343–1400)

Chaucer's Wife of Bath has a good claim to be the first feminist in literature, and her Prologue is a counterweight to the misogyny of the period. Its account of her five marriages is unprecedented in its frankness about sexual relations, and it soon becomes apparent, as she talks, that she is highly intelligent, keenly argumentative and formidably well read (the last two attributes presumably stimulated by her fifth husband, Jankyn, 'a clerk of Oxenford').

Her relationship with Jankyn (whom she married 'for love, and not riches') began well before her fourth husband's death, and he attended the funeral. This extract is translated from the Middle English by John Carey.

When husband number four lay on his bier,
I looked upset, and squeezed out many a tear,
And hid my face behind my handkerchief,
To show that I felt proper wifely grief,
But truly my regrets were very few,
Because I had a substitute in view.
My old man's funeral was on the morrow,
And all our neighbours came to show their sorrow.
Jankyn, our clerk, was there among the rest,
Nicely turned out, and looking at his best,
And, watching him, I thought he had a pair
Of lovely legs, and feet so neat and fair,
That all at once I lost my heart, though he

Was not much more than twenty – as for me,
I'd not see forty again, to tell the truth.
But then I've always had a taste for youth.
Besides, I am gap-toothed, which people say
Shows that with me Saint Venus has her way.
And so she did, for I was young and fair
And rich and well set up and debonair;
And truly, as my husbands all opined,
My *quoniam* was perfect of its kind.

'Quoniam' was an educated euphemism for 'coney' or pudendum, a usage the Wife presumably picked up from Jankyn. The marriage was stormy at first. Jankyn insisted on reading aloud from a book about evil women, culled from a wide range of learned sources. Exasperated, she tore three pages out, whereupon he punched her on the ear, deafening her. But he repented, and agreed that henceforth she should have the 'maistrie', that is, make all the decisions, and after that they never quarrelled again.

WILLIAM LANGLAND
(1330–86)

Piers Plowman is a great allegorical and mystical poem, probably written around 1379. Its ideas influenced the leaders of the Peasants' Revolt (1381), and its criticisms of the church were taken up by the Lollards. Its persistent theme is the contrast between the rich and the poor. The rich ('wasters') in this extract from the Prologue are corrupt, and the poor labour to grow food for them. In line 20 'played' means 'relaxed'. The translation is by John Carey.

In a summer season when soft was the sun,
I clad me in clothes as I a shepherd were,
In habit as a hermit, unholy of works,
Went wide in this world wonders to hear.
But on a May morning on Malvern Hills
I met with a marvel, a fairy thing I thought,
I was weary of wandering and went me to rest
Under a broad bank by a brook side,
And as I lay and leaned and looked on the waters,
I slumbered into a sleep they rippled so merrily.
  Then I began to dream a marvellous dream:
I was in a wilderness, I knew not where,
And as I looked to the east and high to the sun,
I saw a tower on a hill, beautifully built;
A deep dell beneath, a dungeon therein,
With deep ditches and dark and dreadful to see.

A fair field full of folk   I found between them,
Of all manner of men,   the mean and the rich,
Working and wandering   as the world asks.
        Some set themselves to plough,   and played full
                                                        seldom,
In setting and sowing   they laboured hard,
And won what these wasters   with gluttony destroy.

Will, the dreamer, is instructed about the meaning of goodness by various
teachers in a series of dreams. He learns that corruption is everywhere –
in the church, in the justice system, in commerce. In Passus 2, a character
called Holychurch points out to him the chief culprit.

I looked on my left hand   as the lady taught me,
And was aware of a woman   wealthily clothed,
Flouncing in furs   the finest on earth,
Crowned with a coronet   the king has no better,
Her fingers were finely   fretted with gold wire,
And on them shone rubies   as red as a live coal,
And diamonds of dearest price   and a kind of double
                                                        sapphires,
Pearls and precious beryls   to protect her from poisons.

This, Holychurch tells him, is Lady Meed (meaning 'reward'), and she
corrupts the whole realm, because people will do anything for material
gain.

    Towards the poem's end, Will, still uncertain what goodness is, finds
himself in Jerusalem on Palm Sunday and seems to see Piers, a poor
ploughman, riding into the city on an ass. He asks his companion,
Faith, if this is truly Piers, and Faith explains, in allegorical language,
that Christ has taken on human flesh. *Humana natura* means 'human
nature', *consummatus Deus* 'the most high God', and *deitate Patris* 'the
godhead of the father'.

'Is Piers in this place?' said I,   and he looked at me,
'This Jesus, of his nobility,   will joust in Piers' arms,

In his helm and his hauberk   *humana natura,*
That Christ be not known here   for *consummatus Deus*
In Piers the ploughman's jacket   this jouster will ride.
And no blow will hurt him   as in *deitate Patris*

Will sees Jesus brought before Pilate, and hears the Jews bear witness
against him, saying he has boasted he could destroy the Temple in
Jerusalem and build it again in three days (Matthew 26: 61–2; 27: 40).
Crucifige means 'crucify', *tolle* 'raise him up, i.e. on the cross', and *Ave
rabi* 'Hail rabbi, i.e. teacher'.

'*Crucifige!*', said a catchpole,   'I warrant him a witch'.
'*Tolle, tolle!*' said another and took some sharp thorns
And began with those thorns   a garland to make,
And set it hard on his head   and hailed him in scorn,
Crying, '*Ave rabi!*',   and cast reeds at him.
Nailed him with three nails   naked on the cross.
And poison on a pole   they put up to his lips,
And bade him drink his death-draught,   his days
                                                          were done.
'And if you are so clever,   save yourself now,
If you are Christ and a king's son   come down off the cross,
Then shall we believe that life loves you   and will not
                                                          let you die'.
'It is finished', said Christ,   and began to swoon,
Piteously and pale,   like a prisoner that dies,
The lord of life and of light   then laid his eyes together,
The day for dread withdrew   and dark became the sun,
The veil shook and was cleft   and all the world quaked,
Dead men for that din   came out of deep graves,
And told why the tempest   so long time lasted,
'For a bitter battle',   the dead body said,
'Life and death in this darkness   the one destroys the
                                                          other,
No one shall know truly   who shall have the victory
Until Sunday about sun-rising',   and sank into the earth.

HAFIZ
(c. 1315 – c. 1390)

Not much is known of the life of the great Persian poet Khwāja Shams-ud-Dīn Muḥammad Ḥāfeẓ-e Shīrāzī, known as Hafiz. He was born in Shiraz, Iraq, and is said to have known the Quran by heart as a child. He later lectured on the Quran at a school of theology in Shiraz. He studied Sufism, an Islamic form of mysticism, under a Sufi master, and served as a court poet under several rulers. His lyrical poems, called *ghazals*, use love, wine and women to express the ecstasy of divine inspiration. The nearest approach to this in Hebrew Bible theology is the Song of Songs, often interpreted by Christians as expressing the relationship between Christ and his church.

The translator, Richard le Gallienne, knew no Persian and worked from literal translations. He made no attempt to follow the intricate metrical conventions of the *ghazal*. He titles this poem 'Ode 44'.

ODE 44

Last night, as half asleep I dreaming lay,
    Half naked came she in her little shift,
        With tilted glass, and verses on her lips;
Narcissus-eyes all shining for the fray,
    Filled full of frolic to her wine-red lips,
      Warm as a dewy rose, sudden she slips
Into my bed – just in her little shift.

Said she, half naked, half asleep, half heard,
With a soft sigh betwixt each lazy word,
'O my old lover, do you sleep or wake!'
And instant I sat upright for her sake,
And drank whatever wine she poured for me –
Wine of the tavern, or vintage it might be
Of Heaven's own vine: he surely were a churl
Who refused wine poured out by such a girl.
A double traitor he to wine and love.
Go to, thou puritan! the gods above
Ordained this wine for us, but not for thee;
Drunkards we are by a divine decree,
Yea, by the special privilege of heaven
Foredoomed to drink and foreordained forgiven.

Ah! Hafiz, you are not the only man
    Who promised penitence and broke down after;
For who can keep so hard a promise, man,
    With wine and women brimming o'er with laughter!
O knotted locks, filled like a flower with scent,
How have you ravished this poor penitent!

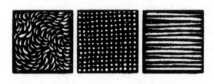

JOHN SKELTON
(c. 1463 – 1529)

'Phyllyp Sparowe' is 'spoken' by Jane Scroop, a schoolgirl living and being educated 'among the Nunnes Black' in the Benedictine convent of Carrow, near Norwich. Jane is mourning the death of her pet sparrow, whom 'Gib, our cat, hath slain'. The Latin interjections give the effect of the nuns singing their offices in the background. *Do mi nus* means 'Lord God', *Levavi oculos meos in montes* is the first line of Psalm 121 ('I lifted up mine eyes unto the hills') and Zenophontes is Xenophon; 'kepe his cut' means 'behave himself', 'prest' means 'quick', 'gressop' is grasshopper and 'slo' is 'slay'.

THE BOKE OF PHYLLYP SPAROWE

Do mi nus,
Helpe nowe, swete Jesus!
Levavi oculos meos in montes
Wolde God I had Zenophontes,
Or Socrates the wyse,
To shew me their deuyse
Moderatly to take
This sorow that I make
For Phyllip Sparowes sake!
So feruently I shake,
I fele my body quake;
So vrgently I am brought

Into carefull thought.
Like Andromach, Hectors wyfe,
Was wery of her lyfe,
When she had lost her ioye,
Noble Hector of Troye;
In lyke maner also
Encreaseth my dedly wo,
For my sparowe is go.

It was so prety a fole,
It would syt on a stole,
And lerned after my schole
For to kepe his cut,
With 'Phyllyp, kepe your cut!'

It had a veluet cap,
And wold syt vpon my lap,
And seke after small wormes,
And somtyme white bred crommes;
And many tymes and ofte
Betwene my brestes softe
It wolde lye and rest;
It was propre and prest.

Somtyme he wolde gaspe
Whan he sawe a waspe;
A fly or a gnat,
He wolde flye at that;
And prytely he would pant
Whan he saw an ant;
Lorde, how he wolde pry
After the butterfly!
Lorde, how he wolde hop
After the gressop!
And whan I sayd, Phyp, Phyp,
Than he wold lepe and skyp,

And take me by the lyp.
Alas, it wyll me slo,
That Phillyp is gone me fro!

Skelton's maverick verse form, now known as Skeltonics, was his own invention, and though it can look like doggerel it was highly sophisticated, varying the number of stresses in the line and using alliteration, parallelism and multiple rhymes.

SIR THOMAS WYATT
(1504–42)

Sir Thomas Wyatt served Henry VIII as a diplomat, but was imprisoned on suspicion of being Anne Boleyn's lover. It is possible he saw her execution, and those of the other suspects, from his cell window. In the atmosphere of terror that Henry created, women put themselves in 'daunger' (danger) if they consorted with someone out of favour, like deer taking bread from a human hand. 'Kyndely' in the next-to-last line is ambiguous, meaning (ironically) 'benevolently' but also 'naturally', since Wyatt believed fickleness natural to women. The sonnet ends, unusually, on a note of doubt: does the woman deserve punishment, or does she not, since she has merely been true to woman's nature?

Note that the woman's punning speech 'dere hart' turns the man into the deer. In line 12 'small' means 'slender'.

THEY FLE FROM ME THAT SOMETYME DID ME SEKE

They fle from me that sometyme did me seke
With naked fote stalking in my chambre.
I have seen theim gentle tame and meke
That nowe are wyld and do not remembre
That sometyme they put theimself in daunger
To take bred at my hand; and nowe they raunge
Besely seking with a continuell chaunge.

Thancked be fortune, it hath ben othrewise
Twenty tymes better; but ons in speciall
In thyn arraye after a pleasaunt gyse
When her lose gowne from her shoulders did fall,
And she me caught in her armes long and small;
Therewithall swetely did me kysse,
And softely said 'dere hert, how like you this?'

It was no dreme: I lay brode waking.
But all is torned thorough my gentilnes
Into a straunge fasshion of forsaking;
And I have leve to goo of her goodeness,
And she also to vse new fangilnes.
But syns that I so kyndely ame serued,
I would fain knowe what she hath deserued.

EDMUND SPENSER
(1552–99)

The main subjects of Spenser's most famous poem, *The Faerie Queene*, are sex and adventure. The sex was, for its time, quite daring. The adventures, by contrast, are strictly moral, illustrating the virtues of holiness, temperance, chastity, friendship, justice and courtesy.

The political reality behind the poem is ugly. Edmund Spenser was in Ireland on the staff of Lord Grey de Wilton, who was responsible for the slaughter of 600 unarmed Irish, Italian and Spanish prisoners at Smerwick in County Kerry, and for a scorched earth policy that caused widespread famine among the Irish. Spenser's *View of the Present State of Ireland* (1596) defends these policies, and the Blatant Beast (*Faerie Queene*, 5.12.37) is invented by Spenser specifically to discredit the accounts of Wilton's atrocities that aroused criticism in Britain. In 1598 Spenser's house in Kilcolman, north Cork, was burned down by Irish freedom fighters and he fled to England with his family, dying soon after.

Spenser is a very uneven poet. Occasional stanzas or half stanzas that, once read, you never forget are held together by stretches of laborious narrative verse. In keeping with the poem's Renaissance credentials, classical references are frequent, as are admiring allusions to artifice. The moral parts of the poem, on the other hand, condemn artifice, because it involves dissimulation and falsity. Classicism and artifice combine, for example, in the tapestry in the House of Busyrane, depicting Leda with Jupiter disguised as a swan.

Then was he turnd into a snowy Swan,
To win faire *Leda* to his louely trade:
O wondrous skill, and sweet wit of the man,
That her in daffadillies sleeping made,
From scorching heat her daintie limbes to shade:
Whiles the proud Bird ruffing his fethers wyde,
And brushing his faire brest, did her inuade;
She slept, yet twixt her eyelids closely spyde,
How towards her he rusht, and smiled at his pryde.

(3.11.32)

Spenser often coins new words and 'ruffing' is one, meaning, it seems, spreading out like a ruff.

Prothalamion, written in 1596 for the marriage of two aristocratic women, refers to the same classical myth when describing two swans floating down the Thames:

The snow, which doth the top of Pindus strew
Did never whiter shew,
Nor Joue himselfe, when he a Swan would be,
For love of Leda, whiter did appeare;
Yet Leda was (they say) as white as he,
Yet not so white as these, nor nothing neare;
So purely white they were . . .

The description of Belphoebe in Book 2 of *The Faerie Queene* combines sexual detailing with invocation of the classical goddess Diana.

And in her hand a sharpe bore-speare she held,
And at her backe a bow and quiuer gay,
Stuft with steele-headed dartes, wherewith she queld
The saluage beastes in her victorious play,
Knit with a golden bauldricke, which forelay
Athwart her snowy brest, and did diuide
Her daintie paps; which like young fruit in May
Now little gan to swell, and being tide
Through her thin weed their places only signifide.

Her yellow lockes crisped, like golden wyre,
About her shoulders weren loosely shed,
And when the winde emongst them did inspyre,
They waued like a penon wyde dispred,
And low behinde her backe were scattered:
And, whether art it were or heedlesse hap,
As through the flouring forrest rash she fled,
In her rude haires sweet flowres themselves did lap,
And flourishing fresh leaues and blossomes did enwrap.

(2.3.29–30)

Among the more salacious sexual episodes is Serena's encounter with some cannibals, who come upon her asleep in a 'wylde desert' in Book 6.

Soone as they spide her, Lord what gladfull glee
They made amongst them selues; but when her face
Like the faire yuory shining they did see,
Each gan his fellow solace and embrace,
For ioy of such good hap by heauenly grace.
Then gan they to deuize what course to take:
Whether to slay her there vpon the place,
Or suffer her out of her sleepe to wake,
And then her eate attonce; or many meales to make.

(6.8.37)

Serena is stripped, allowing Spenser an opportunity to catalogue her 'paps' and other body parts. But Sir Calepine arrives just in time, sees what is happening 'by th'uncertaine glims of starry night' ('glims' is another Spenserian coinage) and slaughters the cannibals.

A purer sex-scene takes place in Book 3 where Chrysogone, tired out from swimming, sunbathes naked and is impregnated by sunbeams, later giving birth to Belphoebe and Amoret, two of the poem's heroines.

Till faint through irkesome wearinesse, adowne
Vpon the grassy ground her selfe she layd
To sleepe, the whiles a gentle slombring swowne

Vpon her fell all naked bare displayd;
The sunne-beames bright vpon her body playd,
Being through former bathing mollifide,
And pierst into her wombe, where they embayd
With so sweet sence and secret power vnspide,
That in her pregnant flesh they shortly fructifide.   (3.6.7)

At the end of the 1590 three-book *Faerie Queene*, Britomart comes upon Amoret and her knight, Scudamour, making love:

Had ye them seene, ye would have surely thought
That they had beene that faire Hermaphrodite,
Which that rich Roman of white marble wrought,
And in his costly bath caused to be site.
So seemd those two, as growne together quite;
That Britomart, halfe enuying their blesse,
Was much empassiond in her gentle sprite,
And to her selfe oft wisht like happinesse:
In vaine she wisht, that fate n'ould let her yet possesse.

(3.12.46)

No one has been able to identify the 'rich Roman', and it has been pointed out that hermaphrodite figures, when they occur in Roman statuary, depict a single bisexual creature, not an embracing couple. So it seems Spenser has dreamed up this gorgeous mix of sex, classicism and artifice – and, as so often, whiteness.

Britomart, mentioned at the end of this stanza, is a warrior who hides her female sex by wearing armour. She is the heroine of Book 3 of *The Faerie Queene*, the Book of Chastity, and, wedded to Arthegal, she is destined to give birth to a line of British heroes, including Queen Elizabeth. Perhaps her envying the bliss of Amoret and Scudamour was thought unseemly for an ancestor of the Virgin Queen, but whatever the reason this marvellous stanza was cut from the 1596 six-book edition of Spenser's poem.

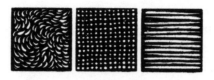

CHRISTOPHER MARLOWE
(1564–93)

Christopher (or Kit) Marlowe was a tragic loss to English poetry and drama. Stabbed to death in a pub brawl in Deptford aged 29, he had been employed in espionage, which may be why he was silenced. *Hero and Leander* is his poetic masterpiece, and its description of Leander's nakedness shows off Marlowe's bisexual sensuality:

> His bodie was as straight as *Circes* wand,
> *Ioue* might haue sipt out *Nectar* from his hand.
> Euen as delicious meate is to the tast,
> So was his necke in touching, and surpast
> The white of *Pelops* shoulder, I could tell ye,
> How smooth his brest was, and how white his bellie,
> And whose immortall fingers did imprint
> That heauenly path, with many a curious dint,
> That runs along his backe . . .

But, apart from *Hero and Leander*, Marlowe's most resplendent poetry is in his plays. This, for example, from *The Jew of Malta*:

> The wealthy *Moore*, that in the *Easterne* rockes
> Without controule can picke his riches vp,
> And in his house heape pearle like pibble-stones:
> Receiue them free, and sell them by the weight,
> Bags of fiery *Opals*, *Saphires*, *Amatists*,

Iacints, hard *Topas*, grasse-green *Emeraulds*,
Beauteous *Rubyes*, sparkling *Diamonds*,
And seildsene costly stones of so great price,
As one of them, indifferently rated,
And of a Carrect of this quantity,
May serue in perill of calamity
To ransom great Kings from captiuity.

Or this fond reminiscence by the murderer Lightborne in *Edward II*:

I learnde in Naples how to poison flowers,
To strangle with a lawne thrust through the throte,
To pierce the wind-pipe with a needles point,
Or, whilst one is a sleepe, to take a quill
And blowe a little powder in his eares,
Or open his mouth, and powre quick siluer downe,
But yet I have a brauer way then these.

Or this clangour of names from *Tamburlaine*, Miltonic before Milton:

Is it not braue to be a King, Techelles?
Vsumeasane and Theridamas,
Is it not passing braue to be a King,
And ride in triumph through Persepolis?

WILLIAM SHAKESPEARE
(1564–1616)

Shakespeare's sonnets are his greatest non-dramatic poems, and much ingenuity has been spent trying to identify the young man to whom they are addressed, the dark lady and the rival poet or poets. But Shakespeare spent his life inventing imaginary situations, and it seems likely that that is what he does in the sonnets. It is noticeable that, as he is careful to make clear in Sonnet 20, perhaps for safety's sake, his interest in the young man is not sexual. Whether this was disingenuous or not, it distinguishes him from Marlowe who was reported as saying openly that 'all they that love not tobacco and boys were fools'.

SONNET 20

A womans face with natures owne hand painted,
Haste thou the Master Mistris of my passion,
A womans gentle hart but not acquainted
With shifting change as is false womens fashion,
An eye more bright then theirs, lesse false in rowling:
Gilding the object where-vpon it gazeth,
A man in hew all *Hews* in his controwling,
Which steales mens eyes and womens soules amaseth.
And for a woman wert thou first created,
Till Nature, as she wrought thee fell a dotinge,
And by addition me of thee defeated,
By adding one thing to my purpose nothing.

But since she prickt thee out for womens pleasure,
Mine be thy loue and thy loues vse their treasure.

Some of Shakespeare's most memorable lyrics are songs from the plays
– Feste's songs 'The Wind and the Rain' and 'Come Away, Death' from
Twelfth Night, for example, or mad Ophelia's song mourning for her
dead father. This one is from *Cymbeline*. In the rather tangled plot of
the play the brothers Guiderius and Arviragus sing it over the grave of,
as they believe, a young boy, Fidele. But Fidele is actually their sister
Imogen, in disguise. Further, she is not dead. The wicked queen
intended to poison her, but a well-wisher replaced the poison with a
sleeping draught.

Feare no more the heate o'th'Sun,
Nor the furious Winters rages,
Thou thy worldly task hast don,
Home art gon, and tane thy wages.
Golden Lads, and Girles all must,
As Chimney-Sweepers come to dust.

Feare no more the frowne o'th'Great,
Thou art past the Tirants stroake,
Care no more to cloath and eate,
To thee the Reede is as the Oake:
    The Scepter, Learning, Physicke must,
    All follow this and come to dust.

Feare no more the Lightning flash.
Nor th'all-dreaded Thunderstone.
Fear not Slander, Censure rash.
Thou hast finish'd ioy and mone.
All Louers young, all Louers must,
Consigne to thee and come to dust.

No Exorciser bar me thee,
Nor no witch-craft charme thee.

Ghost vnlaid forbeare thee.
Nothing ill come neere thee.
Quiet consumation haue,
And renowned be thy graue.

16

JOHN DONNE
(1572–1631)

John Donne is best known for his *Songs and Sonnets*. They set a new standard for love poetry, both by their persistent use of argument and by their changeability. This can show itself even within a single poem. 'Air and Angels', for example, starts with a struggle to find words for the wonder of love at first sight, but ends, insultingly, with the declaration that women's love is less pure than men's.

AIR AND ANGELS

Twice or thrice had I loved thee,
Before I knew thy face or name;
So in a voice, so in a shapelesse flame,
Angells affect us oft, and worship'd bee,
    Still when, to where thou wert, I came,
Some lovely glorious nothing I did see,
    But since, my soule, whose child love is,
Takes limmes of flesh, and else could nothing doe,
    More subtile then the parent is,
Love must not be, but take a body too,
    And therefore what thou wert, and who,
      I bid Love aske, and now
That it assume thy body, I allow,
And fix it selfe in thy lip, eye, and brow.

Whilst thus to ballast love, I thought,
And so more steddily to have gone,
With wares which would sinke admiration,
I saw, I had loves pinnace overfraught,
    Ev'ry thy haire for love to worke upon
Is much too much, some fitter must be sought;
    For, nor in nothing, nor in things
Extreme, and scattring bright, can love inhere;
    Then as an Angell, face, and wings
Of aire, not pure as it, yet pure doth weare,
    So thy love must be my loves spheare;
        Just such disparityie
As is twixt Aire and Angells puritie,
'Twixt womens love and mens, will ever bee.

But Donne is a more versatile poet than even the *Songs and Sonnets* suggest. In a little-known poem called *The Progress of the Soul* he traces the soul of the apple picked by Eve through various occupants. The intention is partly satirical, but Donne shows himself responsive to nature and its processes. The soul enters:

    . . . a small blew shell, the which a poore
Warme bird oerspread, and sat still evermore,
    Till her uncloath'd child kickt, and pick'd it selfe adore.

    Outcrept a sparrow, this soules moving Inne,
On whose raw armes stiffe feathers now begin,
As childrens teeth through gummes, to breake with paine,
His flesh is jelly yet, and his bones threds,
All downy a new mantle overspreads,
A mouth he opes, which would as much containe
As his late house, and the first houre speaks plaine,
And chirps alowd for meat. Meat fit for men
His father steales for him, and so feeds then
    One that, within a moneth, will beate him from his hen.

This sensitive but unsentimental response to nature suggests that Donne might have been a great scientific poet – a thing the English language has never, yet, produced. He was clearly a more scientifically educated poet than any other writing at his time, or long after. His step-father was president of the Royal College of Physicians, and Donne's references to the nervous system suggest he had seen the illustrations in the landmark scientific work *Fabrica* by Andreas Vesalius, the founder of modern anatomy.

Little is known of Donne as a young man, except that he went to the theatre a lot. In the love elegy (Elegy XVII, 'On his Mistress') that begins, 'By our first strange and fatal interview', he addresses his lover, who wants to accompany him on his travels disguised as his page. It is a theatrical idea, reminiscent of, say, Viola disguised as Cesario in *Twelfth Night*. Having dissuaded her, he warns her not to betray the secret of their love in his absence:

> When I am gone, dreame me some happinesse,
> Nor let thy lookes our long hid love confesse,
> Nor praise, nor dispraise me, nor blesse nor curse
> Openly loves force, nor in bed fright thy Nurse
> With midnights startings, crying out, oh, oh
> Nurse, ô my love is slaine, I saw him goe
> O'r the white Alpes alone; I saw him I,
> Assail'd, fight, taken, stabb'd, bleed, fall, and die.
> Augure me better chance, except dread *iove*
> Thinke it enough for me to'have had thy love.

The 'nurse' suggests *Romeo and Juliet*, first staged in the mid-1590s, which young Donne may well have seen.

Donne's own power to enter the mind of another being, as drama-tists do, is shown in another little-known poem, 'Sappho to Philaenis', in which the lesbian Sappho addresses her absent lover:

> My two lips, eyes, thighs, differ from thy two,
>   But so, as thine from one another doe;

And, oh, no more; the likenesse being such,
    Why should they not alike in all parts touch?
Hand to strange hand, lippe to lippe none denies;
    Why should they brest to brest, or thighs to thighs?
Likenesse begets such strange selfe flatterie,
    That touching my selfe, all seemes done to thee.
My selfe I embrace, and mine owne hands I kisse,
    And amorously thanke my selfe for this.
Me, in my glasse, I call thee; But alas,
    When I would kisse, teares dimme mine *eyes*, and *glasse*.

So far as I know, this impersonation of same-sex female love by a male poet cannot be matched in English poetry, either in Donne's time or later. Further, Ovid in *Heroides 15* had written a poem, 'Sappho to Phaon', in which Phaon is a man. Donne deliberately contradicts this classical squeamishness.

Donne can never be satisfied with simplicity. He seeks tangles which his intellect can work at. His sonnet on the death of his wife illustrates this. It argues itself into the position of assuming that God has killed her out of jealousy, wrongly identifying her with the world, the flesh and the devil, though in fact it was her example that led Donne to God. 'More love' (line 9) puns on his wife's maiden name, Anne More.

HOLY SONNET XVII

Since she whom I loved hath paid her last debt
To Nature, and to her's, and my good is dead,
And her soul early into heaven vanished, –
Wholly on heavenly things my mind is set.
Here the admiring her my mind did whet
To seek Thee, God; so streams do show their head,
But tho' I have found Thee, and Thou my thirst hast fed,
A holy thirsty dropsy melts me yet.
But why should I beg more love, whenas Thou

Dost woo my soul for hers, off'ring all Thine;
And dost not only fear lest I allow
My love to saints and angels, things divine,
But in Thy tender jealousy dost doubt
Lest the World, Flesh, yea Devil, put thee out?

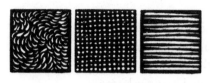

17

BEN JONSON
(1572–1637)

Ben Jonson's most moving poem, for me, is on the death of his son, Benjamin, who died of bubonic plague.

ON MY FIRST SONNE

Farewell, thou child of my right hand, and joy;
>My sinne was too much hope of thee, lov'd boy.
Seven yeares tho' wert lent to me, and I thee pay,
>Exacted by thy fate on the just day.
O, could I lose all father now. For why,
>Will man lament the fate he should envie?
To have so soone scap'd worlds, and fleshes rage,
>And, if no other miserie, yet age?
Rest in soft peace, and ask'd, say here doth lye
>Ben. Jonson his best piece of *Poetrie*.
For whose sake, hence-forth, all his vowes be such,
>As what hee loves may never like too much.

The stern, not to say brutal, God that Jonson imagines here, who will kill a child because his father loves him too much, reflects his own sternness. He was a moralist and satirist at heart, tough and combative. The characters in his great satirical dramas *Volpone* and *The Alchemist* live in a world of prose, unlike the characters in Shakespeare's comedies. Yet Jonson also wrote extravagantly fanciful court masques for

James I and his queen, adorned with delicate poetry such as this hymn
to the moon from *Cynthia's Revels*:

> Queene, and Huntresse, chaste and faire,
> Now the Sunne is laid to sleepe;
> Seated, in thy silver chaire,
> State in wonted manner keepe:
> > Hesperus intreats thy light,
> > Goddesse, excellently bright.
>
> Earth, let not thy envious shade
> Dare it selfe to interpose;
> Cynthia's shining orbe was made
> Heaven to cleere, when day did close:
> > Blesse us then with wished sight,
> > Goddesse, excellently bright.
>
> Lay thy bow of pearle apart,
> And thy crystall-shining quiver;
> Give unto the flying Hart
> Space to breathe, how short soever:
> > Thou that mak'st a day of night,
> > Goddesse, excellently bright.

Jonson's poetic masterpiece, 'To Penshurst', is an idealised portrayal of
the Sidney family house, Penshurst Place, in Kent. It is among the first
'country house' poems, and evolves into an elaborate compliment to
Penhurst's owner, Robert Sidney, Lord Lisle, Sir Philip Sidney's younger
brother. It is typical of Jonson, though, that it starts satirically, describing
what Penshurst is not, rather than what it is. 'Touch' (line 2) is black
marble.

> Thou art not, Penshurst, built to envious show,
> > Of touch, or marble; nor canst boast a row
> Of polish'd pillars, or a roofe of gold;
> > Thou hast no lantherne, whereof tales are told;

Or stayre, or courts; but stand'st an ancient pile,
  And these grudg'd at, art reverenc'd the while.

Jonson knew Penshurst and its estate intimately. He was tutor to Lord Lisle's little son William. As a dependent, he would be expected to flatter – and does, but his flattery verges deliberately on the absurd.

The painted Partrich lyes in every field,
  And, for thy messe, is willing to be kill'd.
And if the high-swolne *Medway* faile thy dish,
  Thou hast thy ponds, that pay thee tribute fish,
Fat, aged Carps, that run into thy net.
  And Pikes, now weary their own kinde to eat,
As loth, the second draught, or cast to stay,
  Officiously, at first, themselves betray.
Bright Eeles, that emulate them, and leap on land;
  Before the fisher, or into his hand.

This account of nature's suicidal determination to serve the Sidney family is of course, a travesty. But the extravagance of the imagining defuses what might otherwise be obsequiousness. The human participants, too, are clearly theatrical walk-ons from some rural idyll, not real seventeenth-century villagers. In fact, the passage is based quite closely on the Roman poet Martial (3.58.33–44):

. . . though thy wals be of the countrey stone,
  They' are rear'd with no mans ruine, no mans grone;
There's none, that dwell about them, wish them downe;
  But all come in, the farmer and the clowne:
And no one empty-handed, to salute
  Thy Lord, and Lady, though they have no sute.
Some bring a Capon, some a rurall Cake,
  Some Nuts, some Apples; some that think they make
The better Cheeses bring 'hem; or else send
  By their ripe daughters, whom they would commend

This way to husbands; and whose baskets beare
    An Embleme of themselves, in plum, or peare.

Towards the poem's end it emerges that Penshurst's perfection serves an overall satirical purpose. It is a house:

Where comes no guest, but is allow'd to eat,
    Without his feare, and of thy Lords own meat:
Where the same beere, and bread, and selfe-same wine,
    That is his Lordships, shall be also mine.
And I not faine to sit (as some, this day,
    At great mens tables) and yet dine away.

This refers to the way Jonson had been treated at Lord Salisbury's house, where the food and drink served to guests of lower rank were inferior to what the host and his friends received. Jonson boasted to the Scottish poet William Drummond that he had reproached Salisbury for this to his face, during dinner.

Complaint, and a stoical refusal to complain, came to Jonson more easily than happiness. They are expressed in 'To the World':

False world, good-night, since thou hast brought
    That houre upon my morne of age,
Hence-forth I quit thee from my thought,
    My part is ended on thy stage.

The poem is subtitled 'A Farewell for a Gentlewoman, virtuous and noble', but it sounds very like Jonson, especially at the end:

No, I doe know, that I was borne
    To age, misfortune, sicknesse, griefe:
But I will beare these, with that scorne,
    As shall not need thy false reliefe.
Nor for my peace will I goe farre,
    As wandrers doe, that still doe rome;

But make my strengths, such as they are,
>Here in my bosome, and at home.

Contempt for the world is central to Jonson's religion, but that does not stop him complaining about how the world conducts itself. In 'To Heaven' it is the way people interpret his piety as illness or dissimulation that offends him:

Good, and great God, can I not think of thee,
>But it must, straight, my melancholy bee?
Is it interpreted in mee disease,
>That, laden with my sinnes, I seeke for ease?
O, be thou witnesse, that the reines dost know,
>And hearts of all, if I be sad for show, . . .

He is so anxious to proclaim his own purity of motive that, by the end, he cannot trust even God to get his behaviour in its correctly innocent perspective:

Yet dare I not complaine, or wish for death
>With holy Paul, lest it be thought the breath
Of Discontent; or that these prayers bee
>For wearinesse of life, not love of thee.

18

ROBERT HERRICK
(1591–1674)

Robert Herrick was the son of a goldsmith, and for six years was apprenticed to an uncle who was a goldsmith and jeweller. Maybe handling precious metals helped to develop his miniaturist poetic style, which depends on scrupulous attention to nuance. By his standards, 'To Daffodils' is quite a long poem.

Ordained in 1623, he became vicar of the parish church of Dean Prior in Devon in 1630, was ejected by the Parliamentarians after the Civil War, but got his living back following the Restoration.

TO DAFFODILS

Fair Daffodils, we weep to see
    You haste away so soon:
As yet the early-rising Sun
    Has not attain'd his noon.
      Stay, stay,
    Until the hasting day
      Has run
    But to the even-song;
And, having pray'd together, we
    Will go with you along.

We have short time to stay, as you,
    We have as short a Spring;

As quick a growth to meet decay
    As you, or any thing.
      We die,
    As your hours do, and dry
      Away,
    Like to the Summer's rain;
Or as the pearls of morning's dew
    Ne'er to be found again.

19

ANDREW MARVELL
(1621–78)

Andrew Marvell is a bewildering poet, and hard to categorise. Driven to choose a single poem as his greatest, I would pick 'The Garden':

THE GARDEN

How vainly men themselves amaze
To win the Palm, the Oke, or Bayes;
And their uncessant Labours see
Crown'd from some single Herb or Tree,
Whose short and narrow verged Shade
Does prudently their Toyles upbraid;
While all Flow'rs and all Trees do close
To weave the Garlands of repose.

Fair Quiet, have I found thee here,
And Innocence thy Sister dear!
Mistaken long, I sought you then
In busie Companies of Men.
Your sacred Plants, if here below,
Only among the Plants will grow.
Society is all but rude,
To this delicious Solitude.

No white nor red was ever seen
So am'rous as this lovely green.
Fond Lovers, cruel as their Flame,
Cut in these Trees their Mistress name.
Little, Alas, they know, or heed,
How far these Beauties Hers exceed!
Fair Trees! where s'eer your barkes I wound,
No Name shall but your own be found.

When we have run our Passions heat,
Love hither makes his best retreat.
The *Gods*, that mortal Beauty chase,
Still in a Tree did end their race.
Apollo hunted *Daphne* so,
Only that She might Laurel grow.
And *Pan* did after *Syrinx* speed,
Not as a Nymph, but for a Reed.

What wond'rous Life in this I lead!
Ripe Apples drop about my head;
The Luscious Clusters of the Vine
Upon my Mouth do crush their Wine;
The Nectaren, and curious Peach,
Into my hands themselves do reach;
Stumbling on Melons, as I pass,
Insnar'd with Flow'rs, I fall on Grass.

Mean while the Mind, from pleasure less,
Withdraws into its happiness:
The Mind, that Ocean where each kind
Doth streight its own resemblance find;
Yet it creates, transcending these,
Far other Worlds, and other Seas;
Annihilating all that's made
To a green Thought in a green Shade.

Here at the Fountains sliding foot,
Or at some Fruit-tree's mossy root,
Casting the Bodies Vest aside,
My Soul into the boughs does glide:
There like a Bird it sits, and sings,
Then whets, and combs its silver Wings;
And, till prepar'd for longer flight,
Waves in its Plumes the various Light.

Such was that happy Garden-state,
While Man there walk'd without a Mate:
After a Place so pure and sweet,
What other Help could yet be meet!
But 'twas beyond a Mortal's share
To wander solitary there:
Two Paradises 'twere in one
To live in Paradise alone.

How well the skilful Gardner drew
Of flow'rs and herbes this Dial new;
Where from above the milder Sun
Does through a fragrant Zodiack run;
And, as it works, th'industrious Bee
Computes its time as well as we.
How could such sweet and wholsome Hours
Be reckon'd but with herbs and flow'rs!

This is a poem that shows Marvell's wit – pretending, for example, that 'palm', 'oke' and 'bayes', all of them symbols of triumph, could be got more easily by just picking them off trees, or pretending that the gods chased nymphs to make them turn into trees, when really the nymphs were turned into trees to allow them to escape from the lustful gods. But 'The Garden' is more than just witty, and its concerns connect it with other poems by Marvell. The soul escaping from the body links it to 'A Dialogue between the Soul and the Body', where the soul complains that it is trapped in the body:

O who shall, from this Dungeon, raise
A Soul inslav'd so many wayes?
With bolts of Bones, that fettered stands
In Feet; and manacled in Hands.
Here blinded with an Eye; and there
Deaf with the drumming of an Ear.
A Soul hung up, as 'twere, in Chains
Of Nerves, and Arteries, and Veins.

But the body complains that the soul fills it with feelings – hope, fear, love, hate, joy, sorrow. Without a soul the body would be innocent, like a tree:

What but a Soul could have the wit
To build me up for Sin so fit?
So Architects do square and hew,
Green Trees that in the Forest grew.

Living innocently in a garden, like a plant or a tree, and not feeling human love, is the idea that hovers behind both poems – and others, 'The Nymph Complaining for the Death of her Faun', for example. It starts as if it will be about war:

The wanton Troopers riding by
Have shot my Faun and it will dye.

But we hear no more about the troopers, and not much about 'unconstant Silvio'. Human love is rejected, as in 'The Garden'. Instead the 'pure virgin' faun and the nymph's garden are the poem's subjects, and the faun strangely turns into the garden:

I have a Garden of my own,
But so with Roses over grown,
And Lillies, that you would it guess
To be a little Wilderness.
And all the Spring time of the year

It onely loved to be there.
Among the beds of Lillyes, I
Have sought it oft, where it should lye;
Yet could not, till it self would rise,
Find it, although before mine Eyes.
For, in the flaxen Lillies shade
It like a bank of Lillies laid.
Upon the Roses it would feed,
Until its Lips ev'n seemed to bleed:
And then to me 'twould boldly trip,
And print those Roses on my Lip.
But all its chief delight was still
On Roses thus its self to fill:
And its pure virgin Limbs to fold
In whitest sheets of Lillies cold.
Had it liv'd long, it would have been
Lillies without, Roses within.

Another 'nymph' who blends with nature, like the faun, appears in 'The Picture of Little T.C. in a Prospect of Flowers' (a poem addressed to a friend's child, Theophila Cornewall):

See with what simplicity
This Nimph begins her golden daies!
In the green Grass she loves to lie,
And there with her fair Aspect tames
The Wilder flow'rs, and gives them names:
But only with the Roses playes;
        And them does tell
What Colour best becomes them, and what Smell.

Escape to a green world is common to all these poems and it is enacted, again, in 'Bermudas'. Here, though, it is given a historical setting. The escapees Marvell imagines are champions of religious freedom, fleeing the punitive regime of Charles I's Archbishop Laud. They find that God has provided an island paradise for them:

He hangs in shades the Orange bright,
Like golden Lamps in a green Night.
And does in the Pomgranates close,
Jewels more rich than *Ormus* show's.
He makes the Figs our mouths to meet;
And throws the Melons at our feet.
But Apples plants of such a price,
No Tree could ever bear them twice.

The 'apples' are pineapples, which Marvell had read about but never seen.

The green world dominates, too, in Marvell's country house poem 'Upon Appleton House', where the poet imagines turning into a plant or a bird:

Thus I, *easie Philosopher*,
Among the *Birds* and *Trees* confer:
And little now to make me, wants
Or of the *Fowles*, or of the *Plants*.
Give me but Wings as they, and I
Streight floting on the Air shall fly:
Or turn me but, and you shall see
I was but an inverted Tree.

All these poems are about different kinds of innocence, and they link innocence to the green world. Reading them requires a historical jump. They are quite unlike nature poetry as it developed in the romantic period and after. Nature in them does not mean wildness, but an escape from wildness. Nature is not peaks and precipices but a garden. It is a space for imagining innocence and linking it with an escape into non-human life.

20

GEORGE HERBERT
(1593–1633)

Almost all George Herbert's poems are about configuring his relationship with God. 'The Flower' is about the periods of doubt and depression when God seems to withdraw from him, or be angry.

THE FLOWER

How fresh, O Lord, how sweet and clean
Are thy returns! ev'n as the flowers in spring;
To which, besides their own demean,
The late-past frosts tributes of pleasure bring.
Grief melts away
Like snows in May,
As if there were no such cold thing.

Who would have thought my shrivel'd heart
Could have recovered greennesse? It was gone
Quite underground; as flowers depart
To see their mother-root, when they have blown;
Where they together
All the hard weather,
Dead to the world, keep house unknown.

These are thy wonders, Lord of power,
Killing and quickning, bringing down to hell
And up to heaven in an houre;

Making a chiming of a passing-bell.
     We say amisse,
     This or that is:
    Thy word is all, if we could spell.

O that I once past changing were,
Fast in thy Paradise, where no flower can wither!
    Many a spring I shoot up fair,
Offring at heav'n, growing and groning thither:
     Nor doth my flower
     Want a spring-showre,
    My sinnes and I joining together.

But while I grow in a straight line,
Still upwards bent, as if heav'n were mine own,
    Thy anger comes, and I decline:
What frost to that? What pole is not the zone,
     Where all things burn,
     When thou dost turn,
    And the least frown of thine is shown?

And now in age I bud again,
After so many deaths I live and write;
    I once more smell the dew and rain,
And relish versing: O my onely light,
     It cannot be
     That I am he
    On whom thy tempests fell all night.

These are thy wonders, Lord of love,
To make us see we are but flowers that glide:
    Which when we once can find and prove,
Thou hast a garden for us, where to bide.
     Who would be more,
     Swelling through store,
    Forfeit their Paradise by their pride.

21

HENRY VAUGHAN
(1621–95)

Henry Vaughan was a Welsh doctor. The Brecon Beacons and the River Usk were his home territory, and he grew up in a Welsh-speaking household. He called himself a 'Silurist', a term taken from the Silures, a pre-Roman Celtic tribe.

He thought of himself as having a misspent youth and was 'converted', he said, by reading George Herbert's poetry. He seems to have fought on the Royalist side in the Civil War, and 'They' in 'They are all gone into the world of light' may include battle casualties. 'Perspective' in the last verse means 'telescope'.

Vaughan's twin brother, Thomas, was an alchemist, and technical terms from alchemy occur in Henry's poems.

THEY ARE ALL GONE INTO THE WORLD OF LIGHT

They are all gone into the world of light!
    And I alone sit lingring here;
Their very memory is fair and bright,
    And my sad thoughts doth clear.

It glows and glitters in my cloudy brest
    Like stars upon some gloomy grove,
Or those faint beams in which this hill is drest,
    After the Sun's remove.

I see them walking in an Air of glory,
    Whose light doth trample on my days:
My days, which are at best but dull and hoary,
    Meer glimering and decays.

O holy hope! and high humility,
    High as the Heavens above!
These are your walks, and you have shew'd them me
    To kindle my cold love.

Dear beauteous death! the Jewel of the Just,
    Shining no where, but in the dark;
What mysteries do lie beyond thy dust;
    Could man outlook that mark!

He that hath found some fledg'd birds nest, may know
    At first sight, if the bird be flown;
But what fair Well, or Grove he sings in now,
    That is to him unknown.

And yet, as Angels in some brighter dreams
    Call to the soul, when man doth sleep:
So some strange thoughts transcend our wonted theams,
    And into glory peep.

If a star were confin'd into a Tomb
    Her captive flames must needs burn there;
But when the hand that lockt her up, gives room,
    She'l shine through all the sphære.

O Father of eternal life, and all
    Created glories under thee!
Resume thy spirit from this world of thrall
    Into true liberty.

Either disperse these mists, which blot and fill
    My perspective (still) as they pass,
Or else remove me hence unto that hill,
    Where I shall need no glass.

22

THOMAS TRAHERNE
(1636–74)

Of the great seventeenth-century religious poets, Thomas Traherne is the least known. He was, however, the most learned. He came from a humble background, the son of a cobbler in Hereford, and studied at Brasenose College, Oxford. A saintly scholar, who gave most of his goods to the poor, he died possessing little but his books. The persistent theme of his poetry is the joy and exuberance of being alive, as in 'The Salutation':

THE SALUTATION

These little Limmes,
These Eys and Hands which here I find,
These rosie Cheeks wherwith my Life begins,
Where have ye been? Behind
What Curtain were ye from me hid so long!
Where was, in what Abyss, my Speaking Tongue?

When silent I,
So many thousand thousand yeers,
Beneath the Dust did in a Chaos lie,
How could I Smiles or Tears,
Or Lips or Hands or Eys or Ears perceiv?
Welcom ye Treasures which I now receiv.

I that so long
Was Nothing from Eternitie,
Did little think such Joys as Ears or Tongue,
To Celebrat or See:
Such Sounds to hear, such Hands to feel, such Feet,
Beneath the Skies, on such a Ground to meet.

New Burnisht Joys!
Which yellow Gold and Pearl excell!
Such Sacred Treasures are the Lims in Boys,
In which a Soul doth Dwell;
Their Organized Joynts, and Azure Veins
More Wealth include, then all the World contains.

From Dust I rise,
And out of Nothing now awake,
These Brighter Regions which salute mine Eys,
A Gift from GOD I take.
The Earth, the Seas, the Light, the Day, the Skies,
The Sun and Stars are mine; if those I prize.

Long time before
I in my Mother's Womb was born,
A GOD preparing did this Glorious Store,
The World for me adorne.
Into this Eden so Divine and fair,
So Wide and Bright, I com his Son and Heir.

A Stranger here
Strange Things doth meet, Strange Glories See;
Strange Treasures lodg'd in this fair World appear,
Strange all, and New to me.
But that they mine should be, who nothing was,
That Strangest is of all, yet brought to pass.

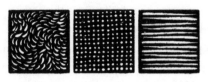

23

JOHN MILTON
(1608–74)

John Milton is not usually thought of as a mystic. But what other word can you use for someone who believed that a female spirit visited him at night and, over the course of several years, dictated to him a long poem, in portions of 40 or so lines at a time? Yet that is what Milton believed about the composition of *Paradise Lost*. His 'celestial patroness', he says:

> ... dictates to me slumbring, or inspires
> Easy my unpremeditated Verse ...   (9.23–4)

Being blind, he could not write down what had been dictated, and when he was waiting for someone to come and do it for him he used to say that he was waiting to be 'milked', as if he thought of himself as female, not just inspired by a woman.

Milton scholars, or male Milton scholars, have always found this embarrassing, and have tried to ignore it, or evade it by explaining that classical poets also claimed to be inspired by a muse and Milton was merely following a 'convention'. But Milton makes a clear distinction, in the poem itself, between his muse and these classical muses. His muse, he claims, is 'heavenly'. She inspired Moses when he wrote the account of the creation of the world in Genesis (*Paradise Lost*, 1.6–10).

How, we may wonder, can Milton know this? Presumably because his muse told him, just as she presumably told him the name he uses to address her, 'Urania'. And this raises the question of how he can know his muse is female. The likeliest answer seems to be that she spoke in a female voice. Public recitals of *Paradise Lost* are usually assigned to men, on the assumption that Milton was the author. But for authenticity they should arguably be allocated to women.

In the other poem where Milton writes of being visited during sleep, the visitor is again a woman – his second wife, Katherine Woodcock, who had died in 1658, after giving birth to a daughter, who also died:

> Methought I saw my late espoused Saint
>   Brought to me like *Alcestis* from the grave,
>   Whom *Joves* great Son to her glad Husband gave,
>   Rescu'd from death by force though pale and faint.
> Mine as whom washt from spot of child-bed taint,
>   Purification in the old Law did save,
>   And such, as yet once more I trust to have
>   Full sight of her in Heaven without restraint,
> Came vested all in white, pure as her mind:
>   Her face was vail'd, yet to my fancied sight,
>   Love, sweetness, goodness in her person shin'd
> So clear, as in no face with more delight.
>   But O as to embrace me she enclin'd
>   I wak'd, she fled, and day brought back my night.

Milton had never seen Katherine. He was already blind when they married. That is why what she looked like is only imagined ('fancied'). *Paradise Lost,* too, was written when he was blind. Did he also imagine what his muse looked like? We cannot know. We know only that he heard her voice – or, rather, we know also that he believed she could protect him.

When he invokes her at the start of Book 7, he feels himself to be in danger. He continues to compose his poem at her dictation, he writes:

> . . . though fall'n on evil dayes,
> On evil dayes though fall'n, and evil tongues;
> In darkness, and with dangers compast round,   (7.25–7)

What dangers? The dates of *Paradise Lost*'s composition, and the order in which the various parts were composed, are unknown. But it is usually assumed that it was written between 1658 and 1663. So the restoration of Charles II, and the brutal revenge taken on those who had signed Charles I's death warrant or connived in his execution, took place while the epic was being written. The bodies of those who had died already were dug out of their graves and hung on gibbets. The living were hunted down, hanged until half dead, taken down and disembowelled while still alive. Their bodies were then chopped into 'quarters' and publicly displayed.

The first four regicides to die in this way were executed in October 1660. Milton was arrested and imprisoned in November. He was in grave danger, and knew it. He had acted as Secretary for Foreign Tongues to Cromwell's government, and written a great Latin work for European consumption defending Charles I's execution. In September copies of his books had been publicly burned by the common hangman. His address to his muse at the start of Book 7 continues:

> . . . still govern thou my Song,
> *Urania*, and fit audience find, though few.
> But drive farr off the barbarous dissonance
> Of *Bacchus* and his revellers, the Race
> Of that wild Rout that tore the *Thracian* Bard
> In *Rhodope*, when Woods and Rocks had Eares
> To rapture, till the savage clamor dround
> Both Harp and Voice; nor could the Muse defend
> Her Son. So fail not thou, who thee implores:
> For thou art Heav'nlie, shee an empty dreame. (7.30–9)

The reference here is to Orpheus, the mythical singer and poet whose music could make rocks and trees follow him. According to the myth he was torn to pieces by a mob of Thracian women during a Bacchic orgy. His mother, the classical muse Calliope, was powerless to save him. But Milton prays to Urania, a quite different kind of muse, no empty classical dream, but real and heavenly, to save him from being torn to pieces, not by Thracian women but by the executioner. What is more, perhaps Urania did save him. At any rate, influential friends, including the poet Andrew Marvell, interceded on his behalf and he was released.

In the Bible story, Eve is to blame for the Fall. Milton cannot change that. But he (or his muse) makes Eve intelligent enough to see how she and Adam can escape what she regards as the worst result of the Fall – that the whole human race, their children, have to die. Milton's intelligent Eve is an astonishing innovation. No one had ever made such an addition to the Bible story before. She suggests to Adam that they should simply not have children. They should refrain from sex, or, if that proves unbearable, they should commit suicide:

> Let us seek Death, or he not found, supply
> With our own hands his Office on our selves;
> Why stand we longer shivering under feares,
> That shew no end but Death, and have the power,
> Of many ways to die the shortest choosing,
> Destruction with destruction to destroy.   (10.1001–6)

Milton's Adam is less intelligent that his Eve, another innovation, and he fails to see that her plan is indeed a foolproof, or Godproof, way to save the whole human race from death. He blusters, and pooh-poohs her proposal:

> . . . doubt not but God
> Hath wiselier arm'd his vengeful ire then so
> To be forestall'd;   (10.1022–4)

But in fact God, however vengeful and angry, could do nothing to stop them, since he has given them free will. To force them to have sex, or go on living, would contradict his own decree. Eve sees this; Adam does not.

Feminist critics have noted that Eve is not, initially, attracted to Adam. She falls in love with a female face – her own, reflected in a pool (4.456–66). Then a 'voice', God's or an angel's, tells her it is just a reflection and that she must come and be 'Mother of human Race', whether she likes it or not – 'what could I doe / But follow straight, invisibly thus led?' (4.475–6), But when she first sees Adam she finds him unattractive – 'Less winning soft, less amiablie milde / Than that smooth watry image' (4.479–80). So she runs away, with Adam pounding after her shouting that she was made from his rib (4.481–5). It is not exactly a love match. And this matters. Because Eve's wish to get away from Adam is the reason for her going off gardening by herself, which gives Satan, in his snake disguise, the opportunity to bring about the Fall. All this, like Eve's suggestion about suicide, is Milton's, or Milton's female muse's, addition to the Bible story of the Fall.

Why read *Paradise Lost*? Answer: because it is different from any poem before or since. To understand that, just read some of it aloud and you will quickly hear that it makes a different, richer, more complicated sound than any other English poem. That is because Milton found his model in the orchestration of Virgil's Latin. It was second nature to him, for he wrote poems in Latin himself as easily as in English. Writing about what was for him the greatest of all subjects, the Fall and the coming of death into the world – answering the question 'Why do we have to die?' – he turned to Virgil, and found a medium that was intricate enough for argument, melodious enough for profound feeling and grand enough for majesty. Not to read *Paradise Lost* is not to know what the English language is capable of. Here, as an example of the expression of feeling, is Adam's internal monologue when he realises that Eve has plucked the forbidden fruit:

> . . . with thee
> Certain my resolution is to Die;
> How can I live without thee, how forgoe
> Thy sweet Converse and Love so dearly joyn'd,
> To live again in these wilde Woods forlorn?
> Should God create another *Eve*, and I
> Another Rib afford, yet loss of thee
> Would never from my heart; no no, I feel
> The Link of Nature draw me: Flesh of Flesh,
> Bone of my Bone thou art, and from thy State
> Mine never shall be parted, bliss or woe.   (6.906–16)

24

JOHN DRYDEN
(1631 – 1700)

John Dryden was an astonishingly prolific writer. Words poured from him – dramas, translations, elegies, prologues, epilogues, religious verse. He once wrote 'thoughts come crowding in so fast upon me, that my only difficulty is to choose or to reject; to run them into verse, or to give them the other harmony of prose'.

By contrast with the metrical variety of the previous age, Dryden perfected the derisive flip-flap of the heroic couplet, illustrated in his portrait of the Duke of Buckingham (Zimri) in *Absalom and Achitophel* (lines 543–62). Buckingham belonged to the 'Merry Group' of Restoration rakes, which included John Wilmot, Earl of Rochester, and it was Rochester who, in 1679, two years before *Absalom and Achitophel* was published, had hired thugs to beat Dryden up in an alley in Covent Garden. The Zimri portrait is Dryden's revenge. He includes Buckingham in the 'herd' of people 'Who think too little, and who talk too much':

> Some of their chiefs were princes of the land:
> In the first rank of these did Zimri stand;
> A man so various, that he seemed to be
> Not one, but all mankind's epitome;
> Stiff in opinions, always in the wrong,
> Was everything by starts and nothing long;
> But, in the course of one revolving moon,
> Was chemist, fiddler, statesman, and buffoon;

Then all for women, painting, rhyming, drinking,
Besides ten thousand freaks that died in thinking.
Blest madman, who could every hour employ,
With something new to wish, or to enjoy!
Railing and praising were his usual themes;
And both, to show his judgment, in extremes;
So over violent, or over civil,
That every man with him was God or devil.
In squandering wealth was his peculiar art;
Nothing went unrewarded but desert.
Beggared by fools, whom still he found too late;
He had his jest, and they had his estate.

For its first readers, *Absalom and Achitophel* was urgently topical. It was a satirical rejoinder to Parliament's attempt to get James II debarred from the English throne. The dispute was bloody and frenzied, and played out on the streets of London. But Dryden's poem has paid the price of topicality and is not much read now.

Similarly, Dryden's mock-heroic satire 'Mac Flecknoe' loses its point for us. For one thing, the poem's targets, Richard Flecknoe and Thomas Shadwell, were familiar components of the literary scene. Flecknoe had died only a few years before, so the poem had a topical sharpness that we miss. It had a jealous sting too. Shadwell was by no means the dullard Dryden pretends. The crackpot scientist Sir Nicholas Gimcrack, in his comedy *The Virtuoso*, is funnier than anything Dryden invented. On the other hand, Dryden was in the right, for Sir Nicholas Gimcrack is a satire on the recently founded Royal Society, of which Dryden was a Fellow. Those who mocked the Royal Society, such as Shadwell, were ignorant of science and failed to see the benefits it would bring:

All human things are subject to decay,
And when fate summons, monarchs must obey.
This Flecknoe found, who, like Augustus, young
Was called to empire, and had governed long;
In prose and verse was owned, without dispute,
Through all the realms of Nonsense, absolute.

This aged prince, now flourishing in peace,
And blest with issue of a large increase,
Worn out with business, did at length debate
To settle the succession of the state;
And, pondering which of all his sons was fit
To reign, and wage immortal war with wit;
Cried, – "'Tis resolved! for nature pleads, that he
Should only rule, who most resembles me.
Shadwell alone my perfect image bears,
Mature in dulness from his tender years;
Shadwell alone, of all my sons, is he
Who stands confirmed in full stupidity.
The rest to some faint meaning make pretence,
But Shadwell never deviates into sense;
Some beams of wit on other souls may fall,
Strike through, and make a lucid interval;
But Shadwell's genuine night admits no ray,
His rising fogs prevail upon the day.

Dryden's most moving poem is 'To the Memory of Mr. Oldham', his tribute to the young satirist John Oldham. Nisus and his friend Euryalus (lines 9–10) are characters in Virgil's *Aeneid*, which Dryden translated. Marcellus (line 23) also figures in the *Aeneid*. He was Augustus's nephew and died young. Aeneas sees his shade in Book VI when visiting the underworld.

TO THE MEMORY OF MR. OLDHAM

Farewell, too little and too lately known,
Whom I began to think and call my own:
For sure our souls were near allied, and thine
Cast in the same poetic mould with mine.
One common note on either lyre did strike,
And knaves and fools we both abhorred alike.
To the same goal did both our studies drive;
The last set out, the soonest did arrive.

Thus Nisus fell upon the slippery place,
While his young friend performed and won the race.
O early ripe! to thy abundant store
What could advancing age have added more?
It might (what nature never gives the young)
Have taught the numbers of thy native tongue.
But satire needs not those, and wit will shine
Through the harsh cadence of a rugged line.
A noble error, and but seldom made,
When poets are by too much force betrayed.
The generous fruits, though gathered ere their prime,
Still showed a quickness; and maturing time
But mellows what we write to the dull sweets of rhyme.
Once more, hail, and farewell! farewell, thou young
But ah! too short, Marcellus of our tongue!
Thy brows with ivy and with laurel bound;
But fate and gloomy night encompass thee around.

25

ALEXANDER POPE
(1688–1744)

Alexander Pope is mostly remembered as a satirist. But that belittles him. He was prodigally inventive and sensuously alive as Dryden and the other Augustan poets hardly ever were. Only Pope could have dreamed up the sylphs who watch over Belinda in *The Rape of the Lock*. Despite its title, this is not a poem about rape. In 1711 an impetuous beau, Lord Petre, then aged 23, caused a scandal by snipping off a lock of a young society beauty's hair. In the poem she is Belinda, but in real life she was Arabella Fermor, aged 16. Wishing to calm hurt feelings and put things in perspective, Pope wrote his poem in the mock-heroic mode. Belinda is guarded by an entourage of fairy beings, called sylphs:

> Some to the sun their insect-wings unfold,
> Waft on the breeze, or sink in clouds of gold;
> Transparent forms, too fine for mortal sight,
> Their fluid bodies half dissolv'd in light.
> Loose to the wind their airy garments flew,
> Thin glitt'ring textures of the filmy dew,
> Dipt in the richest tincture of the skies,
> Where light disports in ever-mingling dyes.

The head sylph warns that any sylph who deserts his post:

> Shall feel sharp vengeance soon o'ertake his sins,
> Be stop'd in vials, or transfix'd with pins;
> Or plung'd in lakes of bitter washes lie,

Or wedg'd whole ages in a bodkin's eye:
Gums and Pomatums shall his flight restrain,
While clog'd he beats his silken wings in vain;
Or Alum stypticks with contracting pow'r
Shrink his thin essence like a rivell'd flow'r.

All these punishments, of course, employ Belinda's beauty aids. 'Pomatum', for example, was perfumed ointment, now called pomade – a horrible thing to get on your wings if you are a sylph. What other poet would bother to seek out the exact word 'rivelled' for the effect of applying an alum styptic, usually used to staunch nicks made in shaving, to the petals of a flower?

At such moments Pope seems to be anticipating surrealism, as he often does in *The Dunciad*. For example:

Thence a new world to Nature's laws unknown,
Breaks out refulgent, with a heav'n its own:
Another Cynthia her new journey runs,
And other planets circle other suns.
The forests dance, the rivers upward rise,
Whales sport in woods, and dolphins in the skies;
And last, to give the whole creation grace,
Lo! one vast Egg produces human race.

This, in Book 3, ridicules what Pope considered the extravagant stage effects created by John Rich at Covent Garden for the pantomimes of Lewis Theobald, the original anti-hero of *The Dunciad*. (Theobald's real offence, it should be said, was to be a better Shakespeare scholar than Pope, and to have identified many errors in Pope's edition of Shakespeare). The last line refers to Rich's mime of hatching from an egg, which was one of his most famous performances.

Colley Cibber, who succeeded Theobald as *The Dunciad*'s anti-hero, also becomes surreal when Pope imagines his authorial labours:

Round him much Embryo, much Abortion lay,
Much future Ode, and abdicated Play;

Nonsense precipitate, like running Lead,
That slipped thro' Cracks and Zig-zags of the Head;

Pope's poetic power lay in continually transfiguring reality, so that everyday occurrences are defamiliarised – coffee-making, for instance, in *The Rape of the Lock*:

For lo! the board with cups and spoons is crown'd,
The berries crackle, and the mill turns round;
On shining Altars of *Japan* they raise
The silver lamp; the fiery spirits blaze:
From silver spouts the grateful liquors glide,
While *China*'s earth receives the smoking tyde:

Lyricism is less often Pope's gift. But when, in *The Dunciad*, he imagines the Grand Tour undertaken by young English gentlemen, an undercurrent of affection seems to run through it, despite the overall satirical intent. Grand Tourists head for the Mediterranean, and Venice above all:

To happy Convents, bosom'd deep in vines,
Where slumber Abbots, purple as their wines:
To Isles of fragrance, lilly-silver'd vales,
Diffusing languor in the panting gales:
To lands of singing, or of dancing slaves,
Love-whisp'ring woods, and lute-resounding waves.
But chief her shrine where naked Venus keeps,
And Cupids ride the Lyon of the Deeps.

Pope seldom wrote about himself, perhaps because it would have given his enemies a target. But in his 'Elegy to the Memory of an Unfortunate Lady', apparently about a purely imaginary woman who kills herself for love, he brings himself in at the end.

Poets themselves must fall, like those they sung,
Deaf the prais'd ear, and mute the tuneful tongue.
Ev'n he, whose soul now melts in mournful lays,

Shall shortly want the gen'rous tear he pays;
Then from his closing eyes thy form shall part,
And the last pang shall tear thee from his heart,
Life's idle business at one gasp be o'er,
The Muse forgot, and thou belov'd no more!

In 'A Hymn Written in Windsor Forest' – written when Pope was only 29, despite its elderly tone – he evidently feels that life has been a disappointment:

All hail! once pleasing, once inspiring Shade,
    Scene of my youthful Loves, and happier hours!
Where the kind Muses met me as I stray'd,
    And gently pressed my hand, and said, 'Be ours!–
Take all thou e'er shall have, a constant Muse:
    At Court thou may'st be lik'd, but nothing gain;
Stocks thou may'st buy and sell, but always lose;
    And love the brightest eyes, but love in vain'!

In fact Pope was a keen participant in the stock market and did quite well, and at the time he wrote his 'Hymn' he was intimate with court society surrounding the Prince and Princess of Wales.

As for love, rumours circulated about his relations with the Blount sisters, Teresa and Martha, daughters of a distinguished Catholic family. Teresa was the same age as Pope, Martha two years younger, and the three met as teenagers. He later quarrelled with Teresa, but stayed close to Martha and left her his books and £1,000, a great sum at the time, in his will. However, his 'Epistle to Miss Blount, on her Leaving the Town, after the Coronation', written in 1714, is primarily addressed to Teresa. Her fancy name was 'Zephalinda', which Pope uses in the poem. But Martha, whose fancy name was 'Parthenissa', seems to be in his mind too. He writes how he stands in a London street, abstractedly thinking of them, until his friend John Gay, author of *The Beggar's Opera*, pats his shoulder and reminds him where he is. 'Chairs' refers to sedan chairs.

So when your slave, at some, dear idle time,
(Not plagu'd with head-achs, or the want of ryme)
Stands in the streets, abstracted from the crew,
And while he seems to study, thinks of you:
Just when his fancy points your sprightly eyes,
Or sees the blush of soft *Parthenia* rise,
Gay pats my shoulder, and you vanish quite;
Streets, chairs, and coxcombs, rush upon my fight:
Vext to be still in town, I knit my brow,
Look sour, and hum a song – as you may now.

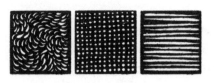

26

SAMUEL JOHNSON
(1709–84)

These two contrasting poems by Samuel Johnson epitomise his moral values.

The first, 'A Short Song of Congratulation', was written to celebrate (though that is hardly the right word) the coming of age of Sir John Lade, who was the nephew of Johnson's friend Mrs Thrale. Lade was a leading figure in Regency society. At 21 he inherited the vast fortune his father had made from brewing. He became famous as a racehorse owner and gambler, and was a close friend of George IV. Mrs Thrale records that when Lade sought Johnson's advice about whether he should marry, Johnson replied, 'I would advise no man to marry, Sir, who is not likely to propagate understanding'. In the event Lade married a woman who was reputed to have been the mistress both of the Duke of York and of an executed highwayman. Together they squandered his fortune, and towards the end of his life he spent time in a debtors' prison.

A SHORT SONG OF CONGRATULATION

Long-expected one and twenty
Ling'ring year, at last is flown,
Pomp and Pleasure, Pride and Plenty
Great Sir John, are all your own.

Loosen'd from the Minor's tether,
Free to mortgage or to sell,

Wild as wind, and light as feather
Bid the slaves of thrift farewel.

Call the Bettys, Kates, and Jennys
Ev'ry name that laughs at Care,
Lavish of your Grandsire's guineas,
Show the Spirit of an heir.

All that prey on vice and folly
Joy to see their quarry fly,
Here the Gamester light and jolly
There the Lender grave and sly.

Wealth, Sir John, was made to wander,
Let it wander as it will;
See the Jocky, see the Pander,
Bid them come, and take their fill.

When the bonny Blade carouses,
Pockets full, and Spirits high,
What are acres? what are houses?
Only dirt, or wet or dry.

If the Guardian or the Mother
Tell the woes of wilful waste,
Scorn their counsel and their pother,
You can hang or drown at last.

Robert Levet (1705–82), the subject of the second poem, 'On the Death of Dr. Robert Levet', was a Yorkshireman who, as a young man, worked as a waiter in Paris at a café frequented by physicians. They noticed him eavesdropping on their conversations and got up a collection for him to train as an apothecary.

Back in London he set up as a doctor, ministering to the poor for modest or no fees. For almost 40 years he had a room in Johnson's house, and met him daily. Boswell records that he was 'grotesque' in appearance, and 'stiff and formal' and 'silent' in company. Johnson admired him greatly, conceding that he could seem a 'brutal fellow', but insisting that his 'brutality' was 'in his manners and not his mind'.

ON THE DEATH OF DR. ROBERT LEVET

Condemn'd to hope's delusive mine,
 As on we toil from day to day,
By sudden blasts, or slow decline,
 Our social comforts drop away.

Well tried through many a varying year,
 See Levet to the grave descend;
Officious, innocent, sincere,
 Of ev'ry friendless name the friend.

Yet still he fills affection's eye,
 Obscurely wise, and coarsely kind;
Nor, letter'd arrogance, deny
 Thy praise to merit unrefin'd.

When fainting nature call'd for aid,
 And hov'ring death prepar'd the blow,
His vig'rous remedy display'd
 The power of art without the show.

In misery's darkest caverns known,
 His useful care was ever nigh,
Where hopeless anguish pour'd his groan,
 And lonely want retir'd to die.

No summons mock'd by chill delay,
 No petty gain disdain'd by pride,
The modest wants of ev'ry day
 The toil of ev'ry day supplied.

His virtues walk'd their narrow round,
    Nor made a pause, nor left a void;
And sure th' Eternal Master found
    The single talent well employed.

27

OLIVER GOLDSMITH
(1728–74)

The Irish poet, novelist and playwright Oliver Goldsmith was a founder member of 'The Club', the circle of notables that formed around Dr Samuel Johnson. He seems to have been an exceptionally likeable man, and wrote two masterpieces, the comedy *She Stoops to Conquer* and the long poem *The Deserted Village*. A phrase that has passed into common use, 'The dog it was that died', comes from his 'Elegy on the Death of a Mad Dog'. His poem, 'When Lovely Woman Stoops to Folly', from his novel *The Vicar of Wakefield*, is probably more familiar than anything else he wrote, partly because T.S. Eliot alludes to it in *The Waste Land*.

In his long poem *The Retaliation* Goldsmith celebrates a dinner party, attended by himself and his friends, in which he associates a particular dish with each of them. Typically he leaves himself to last and appears as 'Magnanimous Goldsmith, the gooseberry fool'. It was agreed that each friend in the poem should write 'epitaphs' for the others. Goldsmith wrote epitaphs for the great actor David Garrick and the portraitist and President of the Royal Academy Sir Joshua Reynolds, both of whom, in the event, long outlived him:

> Here lies David Garrick, describe me who can,
> An abridgement of all that was pleasant in man;
> As an actor, confessed without rival to shine:
> As a wit, if not first, in the very first line;
> Yet, with talents like these and an excellent heart,
> The man had his failings, a dupe to his art.

Like an ill-judging beauty, his colours he spread
And beplastered with rouge his own natural red.
On the stage he was natural, simple, affecting:
'Twas only that, when he was off, he was acting . . .

Here Reynolds is laid and, to tell you my mind,
He has not left a better or wiser behind:
His pencil was striking, resistless and grand;
His manners were gentle, complying and bland;
Still born to improve us in every part,
His pencil our faces, his manners our heart;
To coxcombs averse, yet most civilly steering,
When they judged without skill he was still hard of hearing;
When they talked of their Raphaels, Corregios and stuff,
He shifted his trumpet and only took snuff.

It is said that Garrick immediately said his epitaph was finished, and
recited it impromptu:

Here lies Nolly Goldsmith, for shortness called Noll,
Who wrote like an angel, but talked like poor Poll.

In *The Deserted Village*, Goldsmith laments how the creation of vast
pleasure grounds by the super-rich led to the destruction of age-old
village communities and their way of life:

Sweet Auburn, loveliest village of the plain,
Where health and plenty cheered the labouring swain,
Where smiling spring its earliest visit paid,
And parting summer's lingering blooms delayed:
Dear lovely bowers of innocence and ease,
Seats of my youth, when every sport could please,
How often have I loitered o'er thy green,
Where humble happiness endeared each scene;

Of course this is a ludicrously idealised picture of eighteenth-century peasant life, where pitiless labour and lethal living conditions were the norm. 'Auburn' was a make-believe village, though some have identified it with Nuneham Courtenay near Oxford, which was destroyed and rebuilt so that Earl Harcourt, in 1756, could build a Palladian villa with parkland designed by 'Capability' Brown. Nevertheless, Goldsmith's complaint was justified. The rhythms of rural life were snuffed out, many were made homeless and joined the hordes of emigrants facing an uncertain future in the wilds of America. Goldsmith's denunciation rises to grandeur:

> Ill fares the land, to hastening ills a prey,
> Where wealth accumulates and men decay:
> Princes and lords may flourish or may fade;
> A breath can make them, as a breath has made;
> But a bold peasantry, their country's pride,
> When once destroyed, can never be supplied.

Again, it must be conceded that the 'bold peasantry' is a fiction. Ignorant and uneducated serfs with no civil rights would be nearer the mark. We are reminded that Romanticism, riding on the blood-stained tide of the French Revolution, had to supervene before poetry regained contact with common reality. But that does not mean that Goldsmith was a fraud or bogus. He was of his time, and the indignation expressed in *The Deserted Village* was sincere.

28

JOHN GAY
(1683–1732)

Born in Barnstaple, Devon, and educated by his uncle, the noncon-
formist minister there, John Gay was a friend of Pope, Swift, Johnson
and Congreve. His three-book poem *Trivia* (1716) is written in
mock-heroic style but provides a fascinating guide to London street life
in the early eighteenth century. His subjects in this extract (Book 3,
lines 185–204) are London oyster-women and the French taste for
frogs, snails and the morel, a poisonous-looking mushroom.

Be sure observe where brown *Ostrea* stands,
Who boasts her shelly ware from *Wallfleet* sands;
There may'st thou pass, with safe unmiry feet,
Where the rais'd pavement leads athwart the street.
If where *Fleet-ditch* with muddy current flows,
You chance to roam; where oyster-tubs in rows
Are rang'd beside the posts; there stay thy haste,
And with the sav'ry fish indulge thy taste:
The damsel's knife the gaping shell commands,
While the salt liquor streams between her hands.

The man had sure a palate cover'd o'er
With brass or steel, that on the rocky shore
First broke the oozy oyster's pearly coat,
And risqu'd the living morsel down his throat.
What will not lux'ry taste? Earth, sea, and air

Are daily ransack'd for the bill of fare.
Blood stuff'd in skins is *British* christians food,
And *France* robs marshes of the croaking brood;
Spongy morells in strong ragousts are found,
And in the soupe the slimy snail is drown'd.

Gay's great triumph was *The Beggar's Opera* (1729), a ballad opera in
three acts. Produced by John Rich at his New Theatre in Lincoln's Inn
Fields, it was said to have made Rich gay and Gay rich. Its villain, the
master-criminal Peachum, was a satire on Sir Robert Walpole and his
corrupt ministry. Its hero, the highwayman Macheath, is adored by
Peachum's daughter, Polly, and their love-duet, set to the traditional
tune 'Over the Hills and Far Away', was one of the *Opera*'s most popular
songs:

> Were I laid on Greenland's coast,
>   And in my arms embrac'd my lass;
> Warm amidst eternal frost,
>   Too soon the half year's night would pass.
> Were I sold on Indian soil,
>   Soon as the burning day was clos'd,
> I could mock the sultry toil,
>   When on my charmer's breast repos'd.
> And I would love you all the day,
> Every night would kiss and play,
> If with me you'd fondly stray
> Over the hills and far away.

Gay was buried in Westminster Abbey, with an epitaph by Pope, under
which was inscribed his own epitaph:

> Life is a jest; and all things show it,
> I thought so once; but now I know it.

PHILLIS WHEATLEY
(1753–84)

Phillis Wheatley, the first known African-American woman poet, was born in West Africa and sold into slavery at the age of seven. She was bought and educated by a wealthy Boston family, the Wheatleys, who gave her their name. She was reading Greek and Latin classics by the age of 12, and began writing poetry at 14. In 1774 she came to England with a member of the Wheatley family, was welcomed by leading figures in the London establishment and published a volume of poems that she had been unable to find a publisher for in Boston. She became a devout Christian while living with the Wheatleys, and in her most famous poem she admonishes co-religionists.

ON BEING BROUGHT FROM AFRICA TO AMERICA

'Twas mercy brought me from my *Pagan* land,
Taught my benighted soul to understand
That there's a God, that there's a *Saviour* too:
Once I redemption neither sought nor knew.
Some view our sable race with scornful eye,
'Their colour is a diabolic dye'.
Remember, *Christians*, *Negros*, black as *Cain*,
May be refin'd, and join th'angelic train.

STEPHEN DUCK
(c. 1705–56)

Stephen Duck was born in Wiltshire, into the lowest level of eighteenth-century society, a family of farm labourers. The birthdates of such people were not thought worth recording, and his is unknown. He left charity school at 13 and began life as a labourer. But he was keen to continue his education, and was encouraged by the village squire and schoolmaster, and by a cleric, Alured Clarke, later dean of Exeter, who introduced him into London society.

His *Poems* (1736) counted Pope and Swift among its subscribers, and Queen Caroline granted him an annuity. But her death in 1737 left him without a patron. Ordained in 1746, he became rector of Byfleet in Surrey. This ascent through the class barriers of eighteenth-century society would be hard to parallel and the consequent strain evidently caused a breakdown. In 1756 he took his own life.

Duck's poem 'The Thresher's Labour' (1730) was celebrated among the literary set in London. Threshing was done by hand in the eighteenth century, using a 'threshal', a two-handed flail, consisting of a stick with a club attached to the end by a chain, which had not changed essentially since medieval times. The work was extremely arduous, and it is estimated that in terms of working hours threshing accounted for a quarter of all agricultural labour before the invention of threshing machines. 'Winnowing', the last stage in grain production, meant removing the chaff from the grain by blowing a current of air through it. After that, the grain could be weighed and the harvest estimated.

In this extract from 'The Thresher's Labour' (lines 64–81), 'corn' in the last line means wheat, not maize:

The Sweat, the Dust, and suffocating Smoak,
Make us so much like *Ethiopians* look,
We scare our Wives, when Ev'ning brings us home;
And frighted infants think the Bugbear come.
Week after Week, we this dull Task pursue,
Unless when winn'wing Days produce a new:
A new, indeed, but frequently a worse!
The Threshal yields but to the Master's Curse.
He counts the Bushels, counts how much a Day;
Then swears we've idled half our Time away:
'Why, look ye, Rogues, d'ye think that this will do?
Your Neighbours thresh as much again as you.'
Now in our Hands we wish our noisy Tools,
To drown the hated Names of Rogues and Fools.
But wanting these, we just like School-boys look,
When angry Masters view the blotted Book:
They cry, 'their Ink was faulty, and their Pen;'
We, 'The Corn threshes bad, 'twas cut too green.'

Duck's poem brings home not only the crippling physical effort and the primitive working conditions, but the labourers' sensitivity and shame. They are made to feel like schoolchildren by their employer's insults, and they wish they had their threshing flails back in their hands. For a moment you think, as you read, that they want their flails back so that they can beat their mean-minded and abusive employer. But that might have looked like incitement to violence, so Duck implies it without actually saying it. The idea that the labouring class had feelings that deserved to be respected would be hard to match before the arrival of Romanticism, and unlike the Romantics Duck has first-hand knowledge of what he describes.

31

JOHN CLARE
(1798–1864)

A farm labourer's son, John Clare was born in Helpston, Northamptonshire, and attended the village school till he was 12. In his early years he had various jobs besides labouring. He worked as a potboy in a pub, a gardener (for a nobleman who later gave him financial support) and a lime burner. He also enlisted in the militia, and camped for a time with gypsies. He published his first book of poems in 1820, and another in 1821, and they were highly praised. In 1820 he married a milkmaid, Patty Turner, who bore him seven children.

Despite his early success as a poet, he suffered increasingly from depression and became prey to alarming delusions. In 1837 he entered a private asylum, in hope of a cure, but none was found, and from 1841 to his death he was a patient in Northampton General Lunatic Asylum.

His poems reveal a precise knowledge of the countryside and its creatures – birds, animals, insects – more realistic than anything to be found in the Romantic poets. This, from 'The Nightingale's Nest', for example:

Up this green woodland ride let's softly rove
And list' the nightingale – she dwelleth here
Hush, let the wood-gate softly clap – for fear
The noise might drive her from her home of love
For here I've heard her many a merry year
At morn and eve nay all the live-long day
As though she lived on song – this very spot

Just where that old man's beard all wildly trails
Rude arbours o'er the rode and stops the way
And where that child its blue bell flowers hath got
Laughing and creeping through the mossy rails
There have I hunted like a very boy
Creeping on hands and knees through matted thorns
To find her nest and see her feed her young
And vainly did I many hours employ
All seemed as hidden as a thought unborn
And where these crimping fern-leaves ramp among
The hazel's underboughs Ive nestled down
And watched her while she sung and her renown
Hath made me marvel that so famed a bird
Should have no better dress then russet brown
Her wings would tremble in her extacy
And feathers stand on end as 'twere with joy
And mouth wide open to release her heart
Of its out-sobbing songs . . .

Clare's view of nature is not sentimental ('Badger' is about a badger being hunted to death), but it is merciful. Witness 'Mouse's Nest', which brings Robert Burns's mouse to mind.

MOUSE'S NEST

I found a ball of grass among the hay
And progged it as I passed and went away;
And when I looked I fancied something stirred,
And turned agen and hoped to catch the bird –
When out an old mouse bolted in the wheats
With all her young ones hanging at her teats;
She looked so odd and so grotesque to me,
I ran and wondered what the thing could be,
And pushed the knapweed bunches where I stood;
Then the mouse hurried from the craking brood.

The young ones squeaked, and as I went away
She found her nest again among the hay.
The water o'er the pebbles scarce could run
And broad old cesspools glittered in the sun.

'Progged' (prodded) and 'craking' (crying) are Northants dialect, which Clare often prefers to standard English. The last two lines have been criticised as inconsequential. But they convey facts vital to a countryman, the time of year and the weather – a hot summer's day, almost a drought.

In poetry, sheep and shepherds had for centuries symbolised idyllic pastoral life. Clare reveals the raw reality in 'Sheep in Winter'. 'Pecks' (line 5) is Northants dialect for 'digs'. The absence of punctuation is true to Clare's manuscript.

SHEEP IN WINTER

The sheep get up and make their many tracks
And bear a load of snow upon their backs
And gnaw the frozen turnip to the ground
With sharp quick bite and then go noising round
The boy that pecks the turnips all the day
And knocks his hands to keep the cold away
And laps his legs in straw to keep them warm
And hides behind the hedges from the storm
The sheep as tame as dogs go where he goes
And try to shake their fleeces from the snows
Then leave their frozen meal and wander round
The stubble stack that stands beside the ground
And lye all night and face the drizzling storm
And shun the hovel where they might be warm

While Clare was in the Northampton General Lunatic Asylum, he wrote what for many is his greatest poem, 'I Am':

I AM

I am – yet what I am, none cares or knows;
    My friends forsake me like a memory lost:
I am the self-consumer of my woes –
    They rise and vanish in oblivion's host,
Like shadows in love-frenzied stifled throes
    And yet I am, and live – like vapours tost

Into the nothingness of scorn and noise,
    Into the living sea of waking dreams,
Where there is neither sense of life or joys,
    But the vast shipwreck of my life's esteems;
Even the dearest that I love the best
    Are strange – nay, rather, stranger than the rest.

I long for scenes where man has never trod
    A place where woman never smiled or wept
There to abide with my Creator, God,
    And sleep as I in childhood sweetly slept,
Untroubling and untroubled where I lie
    The grass below – above, the vaulted sky.

32

WILLIAM COWPER
(1731 – 1800)

Fashions in poetry change. William Cowper's six-book poem *The Task* (1785) was admired by Robert Burns, Jane Austen, Samuel Taylor Coleridge and William Wordsworth, among others. Now it is unreadable. Its blank verse seems flaccid, its poetic diction lax and facile. For us, Cowper achieves poetic power most clearly in the poems he wrote during or immediately after his descents into madness, expressing his terror of eternal damnation, and, to a degree, in the religious poems he wrote during his periods of recovery.

The son of the rector of the parish church of Berkhamsted, Hertfordshire, he lost his mother when he was six, and never fully recovered from her death. At Westminster School he developed a deep attachment to the Greek and Latin classics, and later in life translated the *Iliad* and the *Odyssey* into English. In 1763 he fell in love with his cousin, but her father refused to allow the match on the grounds of their blood relationship. This prompted his first period of insanity, during which he attempted suicide three times and was confined to a private asylum. After one of his suicide attempts he wrote what has become one of his best-known poems. It is in the classical metre known as Sapphics, because it was first used by the Greek poet Sappho.

HATRED AND VENGEANCE, MY ETERNAL PORTION

> Hatred and vengeance, my eternal portion,
> Scarce can endure delay of execution,

Wait, with impatient readiness, to seize my
        Soul in a moment.

Damned below Judas: more abhorred than he was,
Who for a few pence sold his holy master.
Twice betrayed, Jesus me, the last delinquent,
        Deems the profanest.

Man disavows, and Deity disowns me:
Hell might afford my miseries a shelter;
Therefore hell keeps her ever-hungry mouths all
        Bolted against me.

Hard lot! encompassed with a thousand dangers;
Weary, faint, trembling with a thousand terrors,
I'm called, if vanquished, to receive a sentence
        Worse than Abiram's.

Him the vindictive rod of angry justice
Sent quick and howling to the centre headlong;
I, fed with judgment, in a fleshly tomb, am
        Buried above ground.

In the Old Testament (Numbers 16: 1–35), Abiram (line 16) and others conspire against Moses and Aaron. He and all the conspirators, along with their families and possessions, are swallowed up by the earth.

After his recovery, Cowper went to live with a retired clergyman, Morley Unwin, and his wife Mary. In 1773, Mary nursed Cowper during another period of insanity, following a dream that renewed his belief that he was eternally damned. They moved to Olney, a market town in Buckinghamshire, where Cowper met John Newton, author of 'Amazing Grace', and together they published the *Olney Hymns* in 1779. Cowper's best-known contribution to the volume reads like an answer to his own terrors.

LIGHT SHINING OUT OF DARKNESS

God moves in a mysterious way
    His wonders to perform;
He plants his footsteps in the sea,
    And rides upon the storm.

Deep in unfathomable mines
    Of never-failing skill,
He treasures up his bright designs,
    And works his sovereign will.

Ye fearful saints, fresh courage take,
    The clouds ye so much dread
Are big with mercy, and shall break
    In blessings on your head.

Judge not the Lord by feeble sense,
    But trust him for his grace;
Behind a frowning providence
    He hides a smiling face.

His purposes will ripen fast,
    Unfolding every hour;
The bud may have a bitter taste,
    But sweet will be the flower.

Blind unbelief is sure to err,
    And scan his work in vain:
God is his own interpreter,
    And He will make it plain.

Mary Unwin died in 1796, and Cowper, it seems, sank again into depression, which is expressed in 'The Castaway', the last poem he published before his death. It is based on a passage in George Anson's *Voyage Around the World*, which tells of a crewman being washed overboard, and the horror of his shipmates as they watched him drown without being able to help:

> He shouted: nor his friends had fail'd
> 　　To check the vessel's course,
> But so the furious blast prevail'd,
> 　　That pitiless perforce,
> They left their outcast mate behind,
> And scudded still before the wind.

Cowper's poem acknowledges its source:

> No poet wept him; but the page
> 　　Of narrative sincere,
> That tells his name, his worth, his age,
> 　　Is wet with Anson's tear.

The poem's final stanza, with a degree of self-concern that may shock modern readers, seems to claim that Cowper's fate is more cruel than the doomed sailor's:

> No voice divine the storm allay'd,
> 　　No light propitious shone,
> When, snatch'd from all effectual aid,
> 　　We perish'd, each alone:
> But I beneath a deeper sea,
> And whelm'd in deeper gulfs than he.

33

THOMAS GRAY
(1716–71)

Thomas Gray can sometimes read like a Romantic poet. His lines in the 'Ode on a Distant Prospect of Eton College', 'Alas, regardless of their doom, / The little victims play!' bring to mind Wordsworth's 'Shades of the prison house begin to close / Upon the growing boy'. The opening of Gray's most famous poem, the *Elegy Written in a Country Churchyard*, suggests sympathy with the working class – the weary ploughman – and an alertness to the sights and sounds of the countryside, and a sense of the poet's aloneness, that we associate with the Romantics. The 'moping owl' could almost have come from Keats:

> The curfew tolls the knell of parting day,
> The lowing herd wind slowly o'er the lea,
> The ploughman homeward plods his weary way,
> And leaves the world to darkness and to me.
>
> Now fades the glimmering landscape on the sight,
> And all the air a solemn stillness holds,
> Save where the beetle wheels his droning flight,
> And drowsy tinklings lull the distant folds:
>
> Save that from yonder ivy-mantled tower
> The moping owl does to the moon complain
> Of such as, wandering near her secret bower,
> Molest her ancient solitary reign.

But as the poem goes on it becomes clear that its portrayal of a typical agricultural worker is absurdly idealised. He is imagined sitting by a 'blazing hearth', looked after by a 'busy housewife' and with healthy, happy children running to welcome him home from his day's work. It is remarkably unlike the worker's lot as described by Stephen Duck. Gray was profoundly learned in several ancient languages and literatures, but it is probable Duck's 'The Thresher's Labour' never came his way.

In the *Elegy* Gray stands up for the poor, and reprimands those who do not. These reprobates are not identified, however, as a Romantic like Shelley would have identified them, but concealed behind inoffensive abstract nouns:

> Let not ambition mock their useful toil,
> Their homely joys, and destiny obscure;
> Nor grandeur hear with a disdainful smile
> The short and simple annals of the poor.
>
> The boast of heraldry, the pomp of power,
> And all that beauty, all that wealth e're gave
> Await alike th'inevitable hour: –
> The paths of glory lead but to the grave.

Though Gray's knowledge of the agricultural working class is evidently limited, he does perceive that they lack education. Towards the end of the *Elegy* a 'hoary-headed swain' addresses the poet and asks him to read an epitaph:

> Approach and read (for thou canst read) the lay
> Graved on the stone beneath yon aged thorn.

The interjection clearly implies that the speaker is illiterate, and Gray realises that huge resources of human potential are wasted because illiteracy is widespread:

> Perhaps in this neglected spot is laid
> Some heart once pregnant with celestial fire;

Hands, that the rod of empire might have sway'd,
Or waked to extasy the living lyre.

But knowledge to their eyes her ample page
Rich with the spoils of time, did ne'er unroll,
Chill penury repress'd their noble rage,
And froze the genial current of the soul.

Full many a gem of purest ray serene
The dark unfathom'd caves of ocean bear:
Full many a flower is born to blush unseen,
And waste its sweetness on the desert air.

Some village-Hampden, that with dauntless breast
The little tyrant of his fields withstood,
Some mute inglorious Milton here may rest,
Some Cromwell, guiltless of his country's blood.

Th'applause of listening senates to command,
The threats of pain and ruin to despise,
To scatter plenty o'er a smiling land,
And read their history in a nation's eyes

Their lot forbad: nor circumscribed alone
Their growing virtues, but their crimes confined;
Forbad to walk thro' slaughter to a throne,
And shut the gates of mercy on mankind.

So Gray decides to look on the bright side. Keeping the working class ignorant and illiterate at least prevents them doing harm. Despite the *Elegy*'s admonitory tone, everything, it seems, may be for the best. The lines about a flower blushing unseen in the desert imply that for the working class to live and die illiterate is really quite natural. Dr Johnson said that the 'Elegy' abounded 'with sentiments to which every bosom returns an echo', and he was right, to a degree. But 'every bosom' is an over statement. If the poem were read aloud to an illiterate eighteenth-century farm worker, he or she would be baffled by phrases such as 'noble rage' or 'the genial current of the soul'. Wordsworth, in the preface to *Lyrical Ballads*, singled out Gray in particular for his 'curiously elaborate' poetic diction.

Gray came from a humble background, and perhaps that made him disinclined to risk offending anyone. His father, a scrivener, was abusive and mentally disturbed, so he lived as a boy with his mother, a milliner. She sent him to Eton, where two of his uncles taught. He was happy there and made several friends including Horace Walpole, the Prime Minister's son, with whom he later went on the Grand Tour, at Walpole's expense. As an undergraduate he went to Peterhouse, Cambridge, but found that the fellows were, as he complained in a letter, 'sleepy, drunken, dull, illiterate Things', so he moved to Pembroke College. But this scornful, derisive side of Gray never gets into his poetry. Or, rather, defiance and denunciation enter the poetry only when the subject is safely in the past. His melodramatic Pindaric ode 'The Bard' is directed against Edward I's war of conquest against the Welsh, which took place in the thirteenth century. The ode ('Ruin seize thee ruthless king!') is essentially a curse uttered by an ancient Welsh bard sitting on a mountain top, and when his curse is over he plunges to his death in the river below. Gray had made it his business to study the history and language of the ancient Welsh. He did not write from ignorance, as he did about his own countrymen. But that made him an antiquarian, not a Romantic.

34

WILLIAM WORDSWORTH
(1770–1850)

Given his later respectability, it seems odd to think of William Wordsworth as wild. But wild he was, both in his ideas and his actions. When he went to France in 1791 it was ostensibly to learn French, but really to escape the dull professions planned for him by his guardian.

In France he became friendly with Michel de Beaupuy, an army officer of noble family but Republican sympathies, who was 15 years Wordsworth's senior. While walking one day they came upon a half-starved country girl, leading a heifer, also half-starved, by a cord attached to her arm. As Wordsworth recalls in the 1805 *Prelude* (9.516–18):

> . . . at the sight my Friend
> In agitation said, ''Tis against *that*
> Which we are fighting,' . . .

It was a turning-point in Wordsworth's life, and converted him to the Revolutionary cause.

Meanwhile, in December 1791 he began French lessons with Annette Vallon, a young woman of Royalist family in Blois, and within months they were lovers. Their daughter Caroline was born in December 1792. But by that time Wordsworth was back in England, leaving Annette's father to sign Caroline's birth certificate in his place. Why did Wordsworth desert Annette and their unborn child? The Revolution was growing more violent, and she would obviously have been safer in England. It looks like irresponsibility – or, again, wildness.

The ideas voiced by Wordsworth in 'The Tables Turned' (*Lyrical Ballads*, 1798) can also seem wild:

> Books! 'tis a dull and endless strife,
> Come, hear the woodland linnet,
> How sweet his music; on my life
> There's more of wisdom in it.

> . . .

> One impulse from a vernal wood
> May teach you more of man;
> Of moral evil and of good,
> Than all the sages can.

> Sweet is the lore which nature brings;
> Our meddling intellect
> Misshapes the beauteous forms of things:
> – We murder to dissect.

> Enough of science and of art;
> Close up those barren leaves;
> Come forth, and bring with you a heart
> That watches and receives.

What exactly can an impulse from a vernal wood teach you about moral evil and good? It is evidently not the right question to ask. Wordsworth is feeling, not thinking. The same is true of 'Lines Written in Early Spring', also in *Lyrical Ballads*. The poet sits in a favourite spot, and meditates:

> Through primrose-tufts, in that sweet bower,
> The periwinkle trail'd its wreathes;
> And 'tis my faith that every flower
> Enjoys the air it breathes.

How can anyone know such a thing? Why should anyone believe it, as Wordsworth says he does? These wild claims do not, of course, devalue the poetry. On the contrary, it was as the wildness drained out of it that the poetry deteriorated.

There is a remnant of it in the 1804 'Immortality Ode' – though Wordsworth regrets that his poetic power has dwindled:

> Whither is fled the visionary gleam?
> Where is it now, the glory and the dream?

> Our birth is but a sleep and a forgetting:
> The Soul that rises with us, our life's Star,
>   Hath had elsewhere its setting,
>   And cometh from afar:
>   Not in entire forgetfulness,
>   And not in utter nakedness,
> But trailing clouds of glory do we come
>   From God, who is our home:
> Heaven lies about us in our infancy!
> Shades of the prison-house begin to close
>   Upon the growing Boy,
> But He beholds the light, and whence it flows,
>   He sees it in his joy; . . .

The strange idea that we existed in some other state, before we were born, is no part of orthodox Christianity. It is one of the last remnants of redeeming wildness in Wordsworth's huge, and increasingly dull, poetic output.

Another remnant comes in the sonnet, 'It is a beauteous evening, calm and free'. This was written at an awkward moment. In 1802 Wordsworth and his sister Dorothy went to Calais to see Annette and her daughter. This was the first time Wordsworth had seen his child, and he wrote the sonnet to commemorate it. It was already arranged that he should marry a childhood friend, Mary Hutchinson, and he did so before the end of the year. But the sonnet does not mention the fact that he is about – in effect – to rob the child of a father and desert

Annette for a second time. For the most part the sonnet is written by
the dull, sanctimonious later Wordsworth. But it comes alive for a
moment:

> Listen! the mighty Being is awake,
> And doth with his eternal motion make
> A sound like thunder – everlastingly.

Who is this 'Being' who is sometimes awake and, presumably, some-
times asleep? Evidently not the Christian God, but some wild idea that
the noise of the sea has put into the poet's head. And it immediately lifts
the poem to sublimity.

What I have called wildness sometimes takes the form of pantheism
or paganism. In the sonnet 'The world is too much with us', written
around 1802, it is once again the sea ('The Sea that bares her bosom to
the moon') that stirs Wordsworth:

> . . . Great God! I'd rather be
> A Pagan suckled in a creed outworn;
> So might I, standing on this pleasant lea,
> Have glimpses that would make me less forlorn;
> Have sight of Proteus rising from the sea;
> Or hear old Triton blow his wreathèd horn.

'Tintern Abbey', written in 1798, contains a pantheist manifesto:

> . . . I have felt
> A presence that disturbs me with the joy
> Of elevated thoughts; a sense sublime
> Of something far more deeply interfused,
> Whose dwelling is the light of setting suns,
> And the round ocean, and the living air,
> And the blue sky, and in the mind of man,
> A motion and a spirit, that impels
> All thinking things, all objects of all thought,
> And rolls through all things. Therefore am I still

A lover of the meadows and the woods,
And mountains; and of all that we behold
From this green earth; of all the mighty world
Of eye and ear, both what they half create,
And what perceive; well pleased to recognize
In nature and the language of the sense,
The anchor of my purest thoughts, the nurse,
The guide, the guardian of my heart, and soul
Of all my moral being.

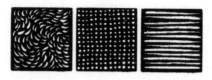

35

SAMUEL TAYLOR COLERIDGE
(1772–1834)

Many would nominate 'Kubla Khan' as the greatest poem in the language. The circumstances that led to its composition (or what Coleridge said they were) are well known. He says that he awoke from an opium dream after reading a book describing Xanadu, the summer palace of the Mongol emperor of China, and had started writing the poem down when he was disturbed by 'a person from Porlock', a nearby village. When the visitor had left, he tried to write the rest of what would have been a 200- to 300-line poem, but could not remember enough of the dream. John Livingston Lowes, in a famous critical study, *The Road to Xanadu* (1927), traced many details in 'Kubla Khan' and *The Rime of the Ancient Mariner* to Coleridge's reading in travel books and elsewhere.

According to Coleridge he had been reading *Purchas his Pilgrimes* (1625) before going to sleep. This was an anthology of various travellers' writings collected by Samuel Purchas, a seventeenth-century clergyman. It has been pointed out that it is unlikely this was Coleridge's bedtime reading. Purchas's book was large (almost 1,000 pages), and also rare and valuable. It is not something Coleridge would have found in, or taken with him to, the 'lonely farmhouse' where he said the poem was written.

It is clear that the poem does not make sense. It would be impossible, for example, to draw a map of the pleasure dome, though many have tried. A 'chasm' that slants down a green hill 'athwart a cedarn cover' is hard to visualise. On the other hand, the poem does make sense to the extent that it is composed of sentences that work grammatically. It is not a collection of random words assembled by free association, as the work of the French symbolist poets at times seems to be. Coleridge was a profoundly learned thinker and critic as well as a poet, and in 'Kubla Khan' he has discovered the space between sense and nonsense where great poetry lies.

KUBLA KHAN: OR, A VISION IN A DREAM. A FRAGMENT

In Xanadu did Kubla Khan
A stately pleasure-dome decree:
Where Alph, the sacred river, ran
Through caverns measureless to man
    Down to a sunless sea.
So twice five miles of fertile ground
With walls and towers were girdled round:
And there were gardens bright with sinuous rills
Where blossomed many an incense-bearing tree;
And here were forests ancient as the hills,
Enfolding sunny spots of greenery.

But oh! that deep romantic chasm which slanted
Down the green hill athwart a cedarn cover!
A savage place! as holy and enchanted
As e'er beneath a waning moon was haunted
By woman wailing for her demon-lover!
And from this chasm, with ceaseless turmoil seething,
As if this earth in fast thick pants were breathing,
A mighty fountain momently was forced:
Amid whose swift half-intermitted burst
Huge fragments vaulted like rebounding hail,
Or chaffy grain beneath the thresher's flail:
And 'mid these dancing rocks at once and ever
It flung up momently the sacred river.
Five miles meandering with a mazy motion

Through wood and dale the sacred river ran,
Then reached the caverns measureless to man,
And sank in tumult to a lifeless ocean:
And 'mid this tumult Kubla heard from far
Ancestral voices prophesying war!
    The shadow of the dome of pleasure
    Floated midway on the waves;
    Where was heard the mingled measure
    From the fountain and the caves.
It was a miracle of rare device,
A sunny pleasure-dome with caves of ice!

    A damsel with a dulcimer
    In a vision once I saw:
    It was an Abyssinian maid,
    And on her dulcimer she played,
    Singing of Mount Abora.
    Could I revive within me
    Her symphony and song,
    To such a deep delight 'twould win me,
That with music loud and long,
I would build that dome in air,
That sunny dome! those caves of ice!
And all who heard should see them there,
And all should cry, Beware! Beware!
His flashing eyes, his floating hair!
Weave a circle round him thrice,
And close your eyes with holy dread,
For he on honey-dew hath fed,
And drunk the milk of Paradise.

36

JOHN KEATS
(1795–1821)

When Keats composed this sonnet is unknown, but it was probably in 1819. Later he copied it out for the young painter Joseph Severn in Severn's copy of Shakespeare's poems (now in the Keats House Museum, Hampstead). Severn accompanied Keats on his voyage to Italy in 1820, where Keats hoped the milder climate would cure his tuberculosis, and he was with Keats when he died on 23 February 1821, aged 25. The sonnet expresses Keats's desperate love for Fanny Brawne. They had met and fallen in love in 1818, and in a letter to her of July 1819, perhaps alluding (in his frequently poor spelling) both to a comet that had been seen in the skies over England that month and the sonnet that he was then composing, he wrote: 'I am distracted with a thousand thoughts. I will imagine you Venus tonight and pray, pray, pray to your star like a Hethen. Your's ever, fair Star'.

SONNET CCXLII

Bright Star! would I were steadfast as thou art –
Not in lone splendour hung aloft the night,
And watching, with eternal lids apart,
Like Nature's patient sleepless Eremite,

The moving waters at their priestlike task
Of pure ablution round earth's human shores,

Or gazing on the new soft fallen mask
Of snow upon the mountains and the moors: –

No – yet still steadfast, still unchangeable,
Pillow'd upon my fair Love's ripening breast
To feel for ever its soft fall and swell,
Awake for ever in a sweet unrest;

Still, still to hear her tender-taken breath,
And so live ever, – or else swoon to death.

37

PERCY BYSSHE SHELLEY
(1792–1822)

One of Shelley's most famous and desolate lyrics has at its heart desertion, loneliness and the death of love.

LINES: 'WHEN THE LAMP IS SHATTERED'

When the lamp is shattered
The light in the dust lies dead –
    When the cloud is scattered
The rainbow's glory is shed.
    When the lute is broken,
Sweet tones are remembered not;
    When the lips have spoken,
Loved accents are soon forgot.

    As music and splendour
Survive not the lamp and the lute,
    The heart's echoes render
No song when the spirit is mute:–
    No song but sad dirges,
Like the wind through a ruined cell,
    Or the mournful surges
That ring the dead seaman's knell.

When hearts have once mingled
Love first leaves the well-built nest;
   The weak one is singled
To endure what it once possessed.
      O Love! who bewailest
The frailty of all things here,
      Why choose you the frailest
For your cradle, your home, and your bier?

      Its passions will rock thee
As the storms rock the ravens on high;
      Bright reason will mock thee,
Like the sun from a wintry sky.
      From thy nest every rafter
Will rot, and thine eagle home
      Leave thee naked to laughter,
When leaves fall and cold winds come.

It is difficult to date this poem, but it seems to have been written early in 1822, and it is tempting to speculate how it relates to desertion and death in Shelley's life. In 1810 he eloped with and married 16-year old Harriet Westbrook. In July 1814 he abandoned Harriet, now pregnant with their son Charles, and travelled to Switzerland with Mary Godwin, daughter of the political philosopher William Godwin. In October 1816 Mary's half-sister, Fanny Imlay, killed herself, possibly because she had fallen in love with Shelley and was distressed by his relationship with Mary. On 10 December 1816 Harriet drowned herself in the Serpentine. She was in an advanced stage of pregnancy. Who the father of her unborn child was is not known, but it was not Shelley.

WILLIAM BLAKE
(1757–1827)

'Ah! Sun-flower' was published in Blake's *Songs of Experience* in 1794.

AH! SUN-FLOWER

Ah Sun-flower! weary of time,
Who countest the steps of the Sun:
Seeking after that sweet golden clime
Where the travellers journey is done.

Where the Youth pined away with desire,
And the pale Virgin shrouded in snow:
Arise from their graves and aspire,
Where my Sun-flower wishes to go.

The poem relates to Blake's belief that repressing emotion warps and distorts life, causing psychological damage. He expresses this most often in relation to sexual desire and its suppression by religion, as in 'The Garden of Love', where:

> ... Priests in black gowns, were walking their rounds,
> And binding with briars, my joys & desires.

In *The Marriage of Heaven and Hell* several of the 'Proverbs of Hell' give extreme expression to the same belief, for example: 'He who desires but acts not, breeds pestilence' and 'Sooner murder an infant in its cradle than nurse unacted desires'.

GEORGE GORDON, LORD BYRON
(1788–1824)

Byron's 'The Dying Gladiator' is an extract from *Childe Harold's Pilgrimage*, Canto 4, stanzas 140–1. It is based on an ancient Roman marble statue in the Capitoline Museum in Rome, depicting a semi-recumbent nude Gaul with a sword wound in his lower right chest. The statue, and particularly the masterly sculpting of the face, became a must-see for young gentlemen doing the Grand Tour. Byron's Grand Tour of 1809–11 did not, however, include Italy, which he first visited in 1816.

> I see before me the Gladiator lie:
>> He leans upon his hand – his manly brow
>> Consents to death, but conquers agony,
>> And his drooped head sinks gradually low –
>> And through his side the last drops, ebbing slow
>> From the red gash, fall heavy, one by one,
>> Like the first of a thunder-shower; and now
>> The arena swims around him – he is gone,
> Ere ceased the inhuman shout which hailed the wretch
>> who won.
>
> He heard it, but he heeded not – his eyes
>> Were with his heart – and that was far away;
>> He recked not of the life he lost nor prize,
>> But where his rude hut by the Danube lay –

There were his young barbarians all at play,
There was their Dacian mother – he, their sire,
Butchered to make a Roman holiday –
All this rushed with his blood – Shall he expire
And unavenged? – Arise! ye Goths, and glut your ire!

40

ROBERT BURNS
(1759–96)

Robert Burns spent his early life as a farm labourer to support his family of siblings. But it did not blunt his sympathy with the weak and helpless. For many, this poem, 'To a Mouse. On Turning Her Up in Her Nest with the Plough, November 1785', is his masterpiece.

In line 4, 'brattle' means 'hurry'; 'whyles' (line 13) means 'sometimes'; 'A daimon-icker in a thrave' (line 15) is an ear of corn in two stooks; 'lave' (line 17) means 'rest'; 'wa's' (line 20) means 'walls'; 'big' (line 21) means 'build'; 'foggage' (line 22) means 'grass'; 'snell' (line 24) means 'bitter' or 'sharp'; 'coulter' (line 29) means 'ploughshare'; 'hald' (line 34) means 'abiding place'; 'thole' (line 35) means 'endure'; 'cranreuch' (line 36) means 'hoar frost'; 'thy lane' (line 37) means 'alone; 'agley' (line 40) means 'wrong'.

TO A MOUSE. ON TURNING HER UP IN HER NEST WITH THE PLOUGH, NOVEMBER 1785

Wee sleekit, cowrin, tim'rous beastie,
O, what a panic's in thy breastie!
Thou need na start awa sae hasty
    Wi' bickering brattle!
I wad be laith to rin an' chase thee,
    Wi' murd'ring pattle!

I'm truly sorry man's dominion
Has broken Nature's social union,
An' justifies that ill opinion
    Which makes thee startle
At me, thy poor, earth-born companion
    An' fellow mortal!

I doubt na, whyles, but thou may thieve;
What then? poor beastie, thou maun live!
A daimon icker in a thrave
    'S a sma' request;
I'll get a blessin wi' the lave,
    An' never miss't!

Thy wee-bit housie, too, in ruin!
Its silly wa's the win's are strewin!
An' naething, now, to big a new ane,
    O' foggage green!
An' bleak December's win's ensuin,
    Baith snell an' keen!

Thou saw the fields laid bare an' waste,
An' weary winter comin fast,
An' cozie here, beneath the blast,
    Thou thought to dwell,
Till crash! the cruel coulter past
    Out thro' thy cell.

That wee-bit heap o' leaves an' stibble,
Has cost thee monie a weary nibble!
Now thou's turn'd out, for a' thy trouble,
    But house or hald,
To thole the Winter's sleety dribble,
    An' cranreuch cauld!

But Mousie, thou art no thy lane,
In proving foresight may be vain:
The best-laid schemes o' mice an' men
    Gang aft agley,
An' lea'e us nought but grief an' pain,
    For promis'd joy!

Still thou art blest, compar'd wi' me!
The present only toucheth thee;
But och! I backward cast my e'e,
    On prospects drear!
An' forward, tho' I canna see,
    I guess an' fear!

41

HEINRICH HEINE
(1797–1856)

Heinrich Heine was partially paralysed eight years before his death, from, it is thought, lead poisoning. The 'Lazarus' poems, written in these years, are considered among his finest. To a friend who praised them he said, 'Yes, I know, they are frighteningly beautiful. They are like a lament from the grave'. This one, 'Wie langsam kriechet sie dahin', is translated by Louis Untermeyer.

WIE LANGSAM KRIECHET SIE DAHIN

How slowly Time, the frightful snail,
    Crawls to the corner that I lie in;
While I, who cannot move at all,
    Watch from the place that I must die in.

Here in my darkened cell no hope
    Enters and breaks the gloom asunder;
I know I shall not leave this room
    Except for one that's six feet under.

Perhaps I have been dead some time;
    Perhaps my bright and whirling fancies
Are only ghosts that, in my head,
    Keep up their wild, nocturnal dances.

They well might be a pack of ghosts,
    Some sort of pagan gods or devils;
And a dead poet's skull is just
    The place they'd choose to have their revels!

Those orgies, furious and sweet,
    Come suddenly, without a warning . . .
And then the poet's cold, dead hand
    Attempts to write them down next morning.

RAINER MARIA RILKE
(1875–1926)

Rainer Maria Rilke moved to Paris in 1902 and acted as secretary to the sculptor Auguste Rodin, about whom he wrote a monograph. Under the sculptor's influence Rilke's style altered from subjective to objective, and he wrote poems based on observation, such as 'Der Panther', which was about the panther in the Jardin des Plantes. This translation is by J.B. Leishman.

THE PANTHER

His gaze those bars keep passing is so misted
with tiredness, it can take in nothing more.
He feels as though a thousand bars existed,
and no more world beyond them than before.

Those supply-powerful paddings, turning there
in the tiniest of circles, well might be
the dance of forces round a center where
some mighty will stands paralyticly.

Just now and then the pupil's noiseless shutter
is lifted – then an image will indart,
down through the limbs' intensive stillness flutter
and end its being in the heart.

ALFRED, LORD TENNYSON
(1809–92)

Death is a persistent theme in Tennyson's poetry, taking forms as different as 'The Charge of the Light Brigade' and 'In Memoriam'. In 'Tithonus' the speaker, doomed to immortality, watches everything wither around him:

> The woods decay, the woods decay and fall,
> The vapours weep their burthen to the ground,
> Man comes and tills the field and lies beneath,
> And after many a summer dies the swan.
> Me only cruel immortality
> Consumes: I wither slowly in thine arms,
> Here at the quiet limit of the world,
> A white-hair'd shadow roaming like a dream
> The ever-silent spaces of the East,
> Far-folded mists, and gleaming halls of morn.

Age and weakness and the search for death recur in 'Ulysses'. The great adventurer of the Trojan War has returned to Ithaca, but finds that peace bores him. He seeks a last voyage:

> The lights begin to twinkle from the rocks:
> The long day wanes: the slow moon climbs: the deep
> Moans round with many voices. Come, my friends,
> 'Tis not too late to seek a newer world.

Push off, and sitting well in order smite
The sounding furrows; for my purpose holds
To sail beyond the sunset, and the baths
Of all the western stars, until I die.
It may be that the gulfs will wash us down:
It may be we shall touch the Happy Isles,
And see the great Achilles, whom we knew.
Tho' much is taken, much abides; and tho'
We are not now that strength which in old days
Moved earth and heaven; that which we are, we are;
One equal temper of heroic hearts,
Made weak by time and fate, but strong in will
To strive, to seek, to find, and not to yield.

Three years before his death, after an illness, Tennyson wrote 'Crossing the Bar'. (The 'bar' is the sand-bar, caused by silting at the mouth of a river, which divides the shallow water from the deep.) 'The words came in a moment', he said, and he asked that it should be printed at the end of all editions of his poems. It clearly reflects his hero's wish in 'Ulysses'.

CROSSING THE BAR

Sunset and evening star,
        And one clear call for me!
And may there be no moaning of the bar,
        When I put out to sea,

But such a tide as moving seems asleep,
        Too full for sound and foam,
When that which drew from out the boundless deep
        Turns again home.

Twilight and evening bell,
        And after that the dark!
And may there be no sadness of farewell,
        When I embark;

For tho' from out our bourne of Time and Place
   The flood may bear me far,
I hope to see my Pilot face to face
   When I have crost the bar.

How far Tennyson believed in the Christian God is disputable. He recorded in his diary, 'I believe in Pantheism of a sort', and wrote in 'In Memoriam' (the poem he wrote in memory of his friend, Arthur Hallam, who died aged 32):

   There lives more faith in honest doubt,
Believe me, than in half the creeds.

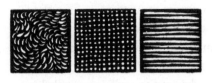

44

ROBERT BROWNING
(1812–89)

Robert Browning's most sinister dramatic monologue is designed to show that love of art and murderous pride are perfectly compatible. The poem 'My Last Duchess' is set in Ferrara and, like Browning's masterpiece *The Ring and the Book,* is based on an actual murder case. Duke Alfonso II of Ferrara married Lucrezia de' Medici in 1558 when he was 25 and she 14. Three years later she died in mysterious circumstances, and poisoning was suspected. Alfonso's emphasis on his 'nine-hundred-years-old name' suggests that he considered the Medicis nouveaux riches. He then courted the daughter of the Holy Roman Emperor, Ferdinand I, who used Nikolaus Madruz, a native of Innsbruck, as his courier. Nikolaus is the visitor to whom the monologue is addressed. The artists Frà Pandolf and Claus of Innsbruck are both fictional.

MY LAST DUCHESS

That's my last Duchess painted on the wall,
Looking as if she were alive. I call
That piece a wonder, now: Frà Pandolf's hands
Worked busily a day, and there she stands.
Will't please you sit and look at her? I said
'Frà Pandolf' by design, for never read
Strangers like you that pictured countenance,
The depth and passion of its earnest glance,
But to myself they turned (since none puts by

The curtain I have drawn for you, but I)
And seemed as they would ask me, if they durst,
How such a glance came there; so, not the first
Are you to turn and ask thus. Sir, 't was not
Her husband's presence only, called that spot
Of joy into the Duchess' cheek; perhaps
Frà Pandolf chanced to say 'Her mantle laps
'Over my lady's wrist too much,' or 'Paint
'Must never hope to reproduce the faint
'Half-flush that dies along her throat:' such stuff
Was courtesy, she thought, and cause enough
For calling up that spot of joy. She had
A heart – how shall I say? – too soon made glad,
Too easily impressed; she liked whate'er
She looked on, and her looks went everywhere.
Sir, 't was all one! My favour at her breast,
The dropping of the daylight in the West,
The bough of cherries some officious fool
Broke in the orchard for her, the white mule
She rode with round the terrace – all and each
Would draw from her alike the approving speech,
Or blush, at least. She thanked men, – good! but thanked
Somehow – I know not how – as if she ranked
My gift of a nine-hundred-years-old name
With anybody's gift. Who'd stoop to blame
This sort of trifling? Even had you skill
In speech – (which I have not) – to make your will
Quite clear to such an one, and say, 'Just this
'Or that in you disgusts me; here you miss,
'Or there exceed the mark' – and if she let
Herself be lessoned so, nor plainly set
Her wits to yours, forsooth, and made excuse,
– E'en then would be some stooping; and I choose
Never to stoop. Oh sir, she smiled, no doubt,
Whene'er I passed her, but who passed without
Much the same smile? This grew; I gave commands;

Then all smiles stopped together. There she stands
As if alive. Will't please you rise? We'll meet
The company below, then. I repeat,
The Count your master's known munificence
Is ample warrant that no just pretence
Of mine for dowry will be disallowed;
Though his fair daughter's self, as I avowed
At starting, is my object. Nay, we'll go
Together down, sir. Notice Neptune, though,
Taming a sea-horse, thought a rarity,
Which Claus of Innsbruck cast in bronze for me!

45

ARTHUR HUGH CLOUGH
(1819–61)

Arthur Hugh Clough's best-known poem, 'Say not, the struggle nought availeth', was made famous by Winston Churchill, who quoted its last two stanzas in a radio broadcast at a dark time in the Second World War. By February 1941 Britain's allies in Europe were all defeated, but the United States was sending Britain armaments, hence the aptness of 'westward, look' in the last line.

SAY NOT, THE STRUGGLE NOUGHT AVAILETH

Say not, the struggle nought availeth,
　　The labour and the wounds are vain,
The enemy faints not, nor faileth,
　　And as things have been, things remain.

If hopes were dupes, fears may be liars;
　　It may be, in yon smoke conceal'd
Your comrades chase e'en now the fliers,
　　And, but for you, possess the field.

For while the tired waves, vainly breaking,
　　Seem here no painful inch to gain,
Far back, through creeks and inlets making,
　　Comes silent, flooding in, the main.

And not by eastern windows only,
    When daylight comes, comes in the light;
In front, the sun climbs slow, how slowly,
    But westward, look, the land is bright.

46

MATTHEW ARNOLD
(1822–88)

Matthew Arnold wrote 'Dover Beach' while on honeymoon in 1851. It has been seen as prefiguring existentialism, in that it represents an individual's quest for authenticity in a seemingly meaningless and absurd world.

In his tragedy *Antigone* Sophocles (line 15) likens the disasters that the gods inflict to the ocean churning up black sand and crashing onto cliffs.

DOVER BEACH

The sea is calm to-night.
The tide is full, the moon lies fair
Upon the straits; – on the French coast the light
Gleams and is gone; the cliffs of England stand,
Glimmering and vast, out in the tranquil bay.
Come to the window, sweet is the night-air!
Only, from the long line of spray
Where the sea meets the moon-blanch'd land,
Listen! you hear the grating roar
Of pebbles which the waves draw back, and fling,
At their return, up the high strand,
Begin, and cease, and then again begin,
With tremulous cadence slow, and bring
The eternal note of sadness in.

Sophocles long ago
Heard it on the Ægæan, and it brought
Into his mind the turbid ebb and flow
Of human misery; we
Find also in the sound a thought,
Hearing it by this distant northern sea.

The Sea of Faith
Was once, too, at the full, and round earth's shore
Lay like the folds of a bright girdle furl'd.
But now I only hear
Its melancholy, long, withdrawing roar,
Retreating, to the breath
Of the night-wind, down the vast edges drear
And naked shingles of the world.

Ah, love, let us be true
To one another! for the world, which seems
To lie before us like a land of dreams,
So various, so beautiful, so new,
Hath really neither joy, nor love, nor light,
Nor certitude, nor peace, nor help for pain;
And we are here as on a darkling plain
Swept with confused alarms of struggle and flight,
Where ignorant armies clash by night.

47

EMILY BRONTË
(1818–48)

Reading this poem you would not guess that Emily Brontë grew up in a close-knit family, sharing pastimes and a fantasy life with her two sisters. Their fantasy life was preserved in the adventure stories they created together, which were based on their brother Branwell's box of toy soldiers. The belief that no one loves her, and that even to want someone to is a kind of immoral corruption, seems a perverse combination of self-pity, self-torment and untruth.

These objections are reasonable. But an alternative way of reading the poem is to see it as an imaginative way of surviving profound adolescent depression. Emily's firm Christian belief ('No coward soul is mine') allows her, in the last stanza, to replace self-pity with self-condemnation, which is active, and puts her back in control, whereas self-pity is passive.

I AM THE ONLY BEING WHOSE DOOM

I am the only being whose doom
No tongue would ask no eye would mourn
I never caused a thought of gloom
A smile of joy since I was born

In secret pleasure – secret tears
This changeful life has slipped away
As friendless after eighteen years
As lone as on my natal day

There have been times I cannot hide
There have been times when this was drear
When my sad soul forgot its pride
And longed for one to love me here

But those were in the early glow
Of feelings not subdued by care
And they have died so long ago
I hardly now believe they were

First melted off the hope of youth
Then Fancy's rainbow fast withdrew
And then experience told me truth
In mortal bosoms never grew

'Twas grief enough to think mankind
All hollow servile insincere –
But worse to trust to my own mind
And find the same corruption there

The firm self-condemnation in the last stanza is achieved, it must be confessed, at the expense of coherent thought. It is not clear why she thinks mankind 'All hollow servile insincere'. Nor is it apparent why she thinks these condemnatory adjectives applicable to herself simply because she once wanted to be loved.

48

CHRISTINA ROSSETTI
(1830–94)

Redemptive love is at the centre of Christina Rossetti's masterpiece 'Goblin Market', where Lizzie saves her sister Laura from the evil goblins. Lizzie's love for Laura is implicitly and daringly likened to the sacrament of Christ's body and blood. In bed together the two young women embrace in perfect union:

> Golden head by golden head,
> Like two pigeons in one nest
> Folded in each other's wings,
> They lay down in their curtained bed:
> Like two blossoms on one stem,
> Like two flakes of new-fall'n snow,
> Like two wands of ivory
> Tipped with gold for awful kings.
> Moon and stars gazed in at them,
> Wind sang to them lullaby,
> Lumbering owls forbore to fly,
> Not a bat flapped to and fro
> Round their rest:
> Cheek to cheek and breast to breast
> Locked together in one nest.

A similar feeling for the female body – Mary's 'breastful of milk' – makes Rossetti's Christmas carol, 'In the bleak mid-winter', different from most carols.

Death is also recurrent in Rossetti's poems. She imagines her own death in 'When I am dead, my dearest' and in 'Remember'.

REMEMBER

Remember me when I am gone away,
  Gone far away into the silent land;
  When you can no more hold me by the hand,
Nor I half turn to go yet turning stay.
Remember me when no more day by day
  You tell me of our future that you planned:
  Only remember me; you understand
It will be late to counsel then or pray.
Yet if you should forget me for a while
  And afterwards remember, do not grieve:
  For if the darkness and corruption leave
A vestige of the thoughts that once I had,
Better by far you should forget and smile
  Than that you should remember and be sad.

She received several offers of marriage, but remained single. At 14 she had a nervous breakdown, and later suffered from depression, which is reflected in 'From the Antique'.

FROM THE ANTIQUE

It's a weary life, it is, she said: –
  Doubly blank in a woman's lot:
I wish and I wish I were a man:
  Or, better than any being, were not:

Were nothing at all in all the world,
  Not a body and not a soul:
Not so much as a grain of dust
  Or drop of water from pole to pole.

Still the world would wag on the same,
    Still the seasons go and come:
Blossoms bloom as in days of old,
    Cherries ripen and wild bees hum.

None would miss me in all the world,
    How much less would care or weep:
I should be nothing, while all the rest
    Would wake and weary and fall asleep.

'Somewhere or Other' expresses what many middle-class Victorian women, confined to the home, and denied the full life that men enjoyed, must have felt.

SOMEWHERE OR OTHER

Somewhere or other there must surely be
    The face not seen, the voice not heard,
The heart that not yet – never yet – ah me!
    Made answer to my word.

Somewhere or other, may be near or far;
    Past land and sea, clean out of sight;
Beyond the wandering moon, beyond the star
    That tracks her night by night.

Somewhere or other, may be far or near;
    With just a wall, a hedge, between;
With just the last leaves of the dying year
    Fallen on a turf grown green.

49

EDGAR ALLAN POE
(1809–49)

Edgar Allan Poe was a central figure in the development of Romanticism in America, and the first American author of note to earn his living by his pen. He is credited with inventing science fiction in his unfinished novel *The Narrative of Arthur Gordon Pym* (1836), and with inventing the detective story in his short story 'The Murders in the Rue Morgue' (1841), where Poe's detective, C. Auguste Dupin, makes his debut. It was printed in later editions of his *Tales of Mystery & Imagination* (1839).

'The Raven' (1845) caused a sensation and made Poe famous. He describes writing it in his critical essay 'The Philosophy of Composition'. This and other critical essays influenced the French symbolist poets, including Baudelaire, whose poems Poe translated.

In 1836 Poe married his 13-year-old cousin, Virginia. She died of consumption in 1847, but showed the first alarming signs of the illness in 1842. This may have influenced 'The Raven'.

The 'distant Aidenn' in the antepenultimate stanza is the Garden of Eden, or Paradise.

THE RAVEN

Once upon a midnight dreary, while I pondered, weak and weary,
Over many a quaint and curious volume of forgotten lore,
While I nodded, nearly napping, suddenly there came a tapping,

As of someone gently rapping, rapping at my chamber door.
"Tis some visiter,' I muttered, 'tapping at my chamber door –
    Only this, and nothing more.'

Ah, distinctly I remember it was in the bleak December,
And each separate dying ember wrought its ghost upon the floor.
Eagerly I wished the morrow; – vainly I had sought to borrow
From my books surcease of sorrow – sorrow for the lost Lenore –
For the rare and radiant maiden whom the angels name Lenore –
    Nameless here for evermore.

And the silken sad uncertain rustling of each purple curtain
Thrilled me – filled me with fantastic terrors never felt before;
So that now, to still the beating of my heart, I stood repeating
"Tis some visiter entreating entrance at my chamber door –
Some late visiter entreating entrance at my chamber door; –
    This it is and nothing more.'

Presently my soul grew stronger; hesitating then no longer,
'Sir,' said I, 'or Madam, truly your forgiveness I implore;
But the fact is I was napping, and so gently you came rapping,
And so gently you came tapping, tapping at my chamber door,
That I scarce was sure I heard you' – here I opened wide the door; –
    Darkness there, and nothing more.

Deep into that darkness peering, long I stood there wondering, fearing,
Doubting, dreaming dreams no mortal ever dared to dream before;
But the silence was unbroken, and the darkness gave no token,
And the only word there spoken was the whispered word, 'Lenore!' –
This I whispered, and an echo murmured back the word, 'Lenore!' –
    Merely this and nothing more.

Back into the chamber turning, all my soul within me burning,
Soon I heard again a tapping somewhat louder than before.
'Surely,' said I, 'surely that is something at my window lattice;
Let me see, then, what thereat is, and this mystery explore –

Let my heart be still a moment and this mystery explore; –
    'Tis the wind and nothing more!'

Open here I flung the shutter, when, with many a flirt and flutter,
In there stepped a stately raven of the saintly days of yore;
Not the least obeisance made he; not a minute stopped or stayed he;
But, with mien of lord or lady, perched above my chamber door –
Perched upon a bust of Pallas just above my chamber door –
    Perched, and sat, and nothing more.

Then this ebony bird beguiling my sad fancy into smiling,
By the grave and stern decorum of the countenance it wore,
'Though thy crest be shorn and shaven, thou,' I said, 'art sure no
    craven,
Ghastly grim and ancient raven wandering from the Nightly shore –
Tell me what thy lordly name is on the Night's Plutonian shore!'
    Quoth the Raven, 'Nevermore.'

Much I marvelled this ungainly fowl to hear discourse so plainly,
Though its answer little meaning – little relevancy bore;
For we cannot help agreeing that no living human being
Ever yet was blest with seeing bird above his chamber door –
Bird or beast upon the sculptured bust above his chamber door,
    With such name as 'Nevermore.'

But the raven, sitting lonely on the placid bust, spoke only
That one word, as if his soul in that one word he did outpour.
Nothing farther then he uttered – not a feather then he fluttered –
Till I scarcely more than muttered 'Other friends have flown before –
On the morrow *he* will leave me, as my hopes have flown before.'
    Then the bird said 'Nevermore.'

Startled at the stillness broken by reply so aptly spoken,
'Doubtless,' said I, 'what it utters is its only stock and store
Caught from some unhappy master whom unmerciful Disaster
Followed fast and followed faster till his songs one burden bore –

Till the dirges of his Hope that melancholy burden bore
    Of "Never – nevermore."'

But the raven still beguiling all my sad soul into smiling,
Straight I wheeled a cushioned seat in front of bird, and bust and door;
Then, upon the velvet sinking, I betook myself to linking
Fancy unto fancy, thinking what this ominous bird of yore –
What this grim, ungainly, ghastly, gaunt, and ominous bird of yore
    Meant in croaking 'Nevermore.'

This I sat engaged in guessing, but no syllable expressing
To the fowl whose fiery eyes now burned into my bosom's core;
This and more I sat divining, with my head at ease reclining
On the cushion's velvet lining that the lamplight gloated o'er,
But whose velvet violet lining with the lamplight gloating o'er,
    She shall press, ah, nevermore!

Then, methought, the air grew denser, perfumed from an unseen
    censer
Swung by angels whose faint foot-falls tinkled on the tufted floor.
'Wretch,' I cried, 'thy God hath lent thee – by these angels he hath
    sent thee
Respite – respite and nepenthe from thy memories of Lenore!
Quaff, oh quaff this kind nepenthe and forget this lost Lenore!'
    Quoth the Raven, 'Nevermore.'

'Prophet!' said I, 'thing of evil! – prophet still, if bird or devil! –
Whether Tempter sent, or whether tempest tossed thee here ashore,
Desolate yet all undaunted, on this desert land enchanted –
On this home by Horror haunted – tell me truly, I implore –
Is there – *is* there balm in Gilead? – tell me – tell me, I implore!'
    Quoth the Raven, 'Nevermore.'

'Prophet!' said I, 'thing of evil! – prophet still, if bird or devil!
By that Heaven that bends above us – by that God we both adore –
Tell this soul with sorrow laden if, within the distant Aidenn,

It shall clasp a sainted maiden whom the angels name Lenore –
Clasp a rare and radiant maiden whom the angels name Lenore.'
     Quoth the Raven, 'Nevermore.'

'Be that word our sign of parting, bird or fiend!' I shrieked,
     upstarting –
'Get thee back into the tempest and the Night's Plutonian shore!
Leave no black plume as a token of that lie thy soul hath spoken!
Leave my loneliness unbroken! – quit the bust above my door!
Take thy beak from out my heart, and take thy form from off my door!'
     Quoth the Raven, 'Nevermore.'

And the Raven, never flitting, still is sitting, still is sitting
On the pallid bust of Pallas just above my chamber door;
And his eyes have all the seeming of a demon's that is dreaming,
And the lamp-light o'er him streaming throws his shadow on the
     floor;
And my soul from out that shadow that lies floating on the floor
     Shall be lifted – nevermore!

50

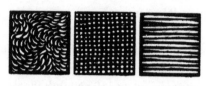

WALT WHITMAN
(1819–92)

Walt Whitman remade American poetry. He sought, through gloriously rambling free verse, to draw the whole nation into his consciousness, and he discarded the old spirit-centred ethic that had dominated poetry hitherto, replacing it with a body-centred one that is generous, inclusive and dynamic.

He hymns the human body in his long poem 'Song of Myself':

I do not press my fingers across my mouth,
I keep as delicate around the bowels as around the head and heart,
Copulation is no more rank to me than death is.

I believe in the flesh and the appetites,
Seeing, hearing, feeling, are miracles, and each part and tag of
    me is a miracle.

Divine am I inside and out, and I make holy whatever I touch
    or am touch'd from,
The scent of these arm-pits aroma finer than prayer,
This head more than churches, bibles, and all the creeds . . .

Whitman was bisexual, having relationships with men but also claiming that he fathered six illegitimate children. The drive to procreate becomes imperious in his poem 'A Woman Waits for Me', to a degree, some may feel, that the woman addressed might resent.

A WOMAN WAITS FOR ME

A woman waits for me, she contains all, nothing is lacking,
Yet all were lacking if sex were lacking, or if the moisture of the
    right man were lacking.

Sex contains all, bodies, souls,
Meanings, proofs, purities, delicacies, results, promulgations,
Songs, commands, health, pride, the maternal mystery, the seminal
    milk,
All hopes, benefactions, bestowals, all the passions, loves, beauties,
    delights of the earth,
All the governments, judges, gods, follow'd persons of the earth,
These are contain'd in sex as parts of itself and justifications of itself.

Without shame the man I like knows and avows the deliciousness
    of his sex,
Without shame the woman I like knows and avows hers.

Now I will dismiss myself from impassive women,
I will go stay with her who waits for me, and with those women that
    are warm-blooded and sufficient for me,
I see that they understand me and do not deny me,
I see that they are worthy of me, I will be the robust husband of
    those women.

They are not one jot less than I am,
They are tann'd in the face by shining suns and blowing winds,
Their flesh has the old divine suppleness and strength,
They know how to swim, row, ride, wrestle, shoot, run, strike,
    retreat, advance, resist, defend themselves,

They are ultimate in their own right – they are calm, clear, well-
    possess'd of themselves.
I draw you close to me, you women,
I cannot let you go, I would do you good,

I am for you, and you are for me, not only for our own sake,
    but for others' sakes,
Envelop'd in you sleep greater heroes and bards,
They refuse to awake at the touch of any man but me.

It is I, you women, I make my way,
I am stern, acrid, large, undissuadable, but I love you,
I do not hurt you any more than is necessary for you,
I pour the stuff to start sons and daughters fit for these States, I
    press with slow rude muscle,
I brace myself effectually, I listen to no entreaties,
I dare not withdraw till I deposit what has so long accumulated
    within me.

Through you I drain the pent-up rivers of myself,
In you I wrap a thousand onward years,
On you I graft the grafts of the best-beloved of me and America,
The drops I distil upon you shall grow fierce and athletic
    girls, new artists, musicians, and singers,
The babes I beget upon you are to beget babes in their turn,
I shall demand perfect men and women out of my love-spendings,
I shall expect them to interpenetrate with others, as I and you
    interpenetrate now,
I shall count on the fruits of the gushing showers of them, as I
    count on the fruits of the gushing showers I give now,
I shall look for loving crops from the birth, life, death, immortality,
    I plant so lovingly now.

51

EMILY DICKINSON
(1830–86)

Emily Dickinson was extremely unlike Whitman, except that they both invented a new kind of poetry. Dickinson's is minimalist, and includes her own system of punctuation and capitalisation. She transcribed her poems (there are about 1,800) in handwritten books. Most of them relate to the inner world of feelings. But this one, 'A narrow Fellow in the Grass' (986), is about the natural world, with Dickinson casting herself as a man who recalls his encounters with snakes as a boy, and the fear he felt.

Massachusetts, where the Dickinsons had their home, has fourteen snake species, of which only two, the timber rattlesnake and the copperhead, are venomous. But some of the harmless snakes resemble venomous species in pattern and behaviour.

A NARROW FELLOW IN THE GRASS

A narrow Fellow in the Grass
Occasionally rides –
You may have met Him – did you not
His notice sudden is –

The Grass divides as with a Comb –
A spotted shaft is seen –
And then it closes at your feet
And opens further on –

He likes a Boggy Acre
A Floor too cool for Corn –
Yet when a Boy, and Barefoot –
I more than once at Noon

Have passed, I thought, a Whip lash
Unbraiding in the Sun
When stooping to secure it
It wrinkled, and was gone –

Several of Nature's people
I know, and they know me –
I feel for them a transport
Of cordiality –

But never met this Fellow
Attended, or alone
Without a tighter breathing
And Zero at the bone –

Another poem about a natural disturbance is 'There came a Wind like
a Bugle' (1593):

THERE CAME A WIND LIKE A BUGLE

There came a Wind like a Bugle –
It quivered though the Grass
And a Green Chill upon the Heat
So ominous did pass
We barred the Windows and the Doors
As from an Emerald Ghost –
The Doom's electric Moccasin
That very instant passed –
On a strange Mob of panting Trees
And Fences flew away
And Rivers where the Houses ran

Those looked that lived – that Day –
The Bell within the steeple wild
The flying tidings told –
How much can come
And much can go,
And yet abide the World!

More commonly Dickinson's poems are about the inner world of feel-
ings, as in this one (393):

DID OUR BEST MOMENT LAST

Did Our Best Moment last –
'Twould supersede the Heaven –
A few – and they by Risk – procure –
So this Sort – are not given –

Except as stimulants – in
Cases of Despair –
Or Stupor – The Reserve –
These Heavenly Moments are –

A Grant of the Divine –
That Certain as it Comes –
Withdraws – and leaves the dazzled Soul
In her unfurnished Rooms

Or this one (1129):

TELL ALL THE TRUTH BUT TELL IT SLANT

Tell all the Truth but tell it slant –
Success in Circuit lies
Too bright for our infirm Delight
The Truth's superb surprise

As Lightning to the Children eased
With explanation kind
The Truth must dazzle gradually
Or every man be blind –

Or this (1774):

TOO HAPPY TIME DISSOLVES ITSELF

Too happy Time dissolves itself
And leaves no remnant by –
'Tis Anguish not a Feather hath
Or too much weight to fly –

52

CHARLES BAUDELAIRE
(1821–67)

Charles Baudelaire may have seen albatrosses when his stepfather sent him on a voyage to Calcutta in 1841, in the hope of curing him of his dissolute habits. This poem, 'The Albatross', translated by Roy Campbell, expresses his sense of the poet as separate from the alien, mocking crowd – a common theme in his poetry.

THE ALBATROSS

Sometimes for sport the men of loafing crews
Snare the great albatrosses of the deep,
The indolent companions of their cruise
As through the bitter vastitudes they sweep.

Scarce have they fished aboard these airy kings
When helpless on such unaccustomed floors,
They piteously droop their huge white wings
And trail them at their sides like drifting oars.

How comical, how ugly, and how meek
Appears this soarer of celestial snows!
One, with his pipe, teases the golden beak,
One, limping, mocks the cripple as he goes.

The Poet, like this monarch of the clouds,
Despising archers, rides the storm elate.
But, stranded on the earth to jeering crowds,
The great wings of the giant baulk his gait.

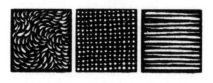

53

DYLAN THOMAS
(1914–53)

This poem, one of Dylan Thomas's most haunting, is about the poet's essential loneliness and isolation. His feeling, however, is different from Baudelaire's. He realises that the people he most wants to write for pay no attention to his poetry, but he does not despise them for it.

IN MY CRAFT OR SULLEN ART

In my craft or sullen art
Exercised in the still night
When only the moon rages
And the lovers lie abed
With all their griefs in their arms,
I labour by singing light
Not for ambition or bread
Or the strut and trade of charms
On the ivory stages
But for the common wages
Of their most secret heart.

Not for the proud man apart
From the raging moon I write
On these spindrift pages
Nor for the towering dead
With their nightingales and psalms

But for the lovers, their arms
Round the griefs of the ages,
Who pay no praise or wages
Nor heed my craft or art.

54

EDWARD LEAR
(1812–88)

Edward Lear was gay, and felt a little sad when friends got married. 'The Owl and the Pussy-cat' gently mocks happy-ever-after love stories.

THE OWL AND THE PUSSY-CAT

The Owl and the Pussy-cat went to sea
    In a beautiful pea-green boat,
They took some honey, and plenty of money,
    Wrapped up in a five-pound note.
The Owl looked up to the stars above,
    And sang to a small guitar,
'O lovely Pussy! O Pussy, my love,
    What a beautiful Pussy you are,
        You are,
           You are!
    What a beautiful Pussy you are!'

Pussy said to the Owl, 'You elegant fowl!
    How charmingly sweet you sing!
O let us be married! too long we have tarried:
    But what shall we do for a ring?'
They sailed away, for a year and a day,
    To the land where the Bong-tree grows
And there in a wood a Piggy-wig stood

With a ring at the end of his nose,
    His nose,
      His nose,
With a ring at the end of his nose.

'Dear Pig, are you willing to sell for one shilling
    Your ring?' Said the Piggy, 'I will'.
So they took it away, and were married next day
    By the Turkey who lives on the hill.
They dined on mince, and slices of quince,
    Which they ate with a runcible spoon;
And hand in hand, on the edge of the sand,
    They danced by the light of the moon,
      The moon,
        The moon,
They danced by the light of the moon.

55

LEWIS CARROLL
(1832–98)

Lewis Carroll (alias Charles Lutwidge Dodgson) wrote the first stanza of 'Jabberwocky' in 1855 to amuse his family, titling it 'Stanza of Anglo-Saxon Poetry'. It read:

Twas bryllyg, and ye slythy toves
Did gyre and gymble in ye wabe:
All mimsy were ye borogoves;
And ye mome raths outgrabe.

This suggests that Carroll had in mind the Anglo-Saxon epic *Beowulf*, in which Beowulf cuts off the monster Grendel's head as the 'beamish boy' cuts off the Jabberwock's. In *Through the Looking Glass*, the sequel to *Alice in Wonderland*, Alice reads the poem in mirror-writing and remarks: 'It seems very pretty but it's rather hard to understand'. Carroll's purpose is mockery of heroic poetry.

JABBERWOCKY

'Twas brillig, and the slithy toves
    Did gyre and gimble in the wabe:
All mimsy were the borogoves,
    And the mome raths outgrabe.

'Beware the Jabberwock, my son!
        The jaws that bite, the claws that catch!
Beware the Jubjub bird, and shun
        The frumious Bandersnatch!'

He took his vorpal sword in hand:
        Long time the manxome foe he sought –
So rested he by the Tumtum tree,
        And stood awhile in thought.

And, as in uffish thought he stood,
        The Jabberwock, with eyes of flame,
Came whiffling through the tulgey wood,
        And burbled as it came!

One, two! One, two! And through and through
        The vorpal blade went snicker-snack!
He left it dead, and with its head
        He went galumphing back.

'And hast thou slain the Jabberwock?
        Come to my arms, my beamish boy!
O frabjous day! Callooh! Callay!'
        He chortled in his joy.

'Twas brillig, and the slithy toves
        Did gyre and gimble in the wabe:
All mimsy were the borogoves,
        And the mome raths outgrabe.

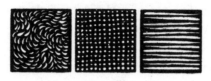

56

CHARLOTTE MEW
(1869–1928)

Charlotte Mew is one of the greatest English women poets, and argu-ably this poem, 'The Farmer's Bride', is her masterpiece. Whether she had any sexual experience is not clear. Two of her siblings suffered from mental illness, so she and her sister renounced marriage for fear of passing on insanity to their children.

THE FARMER'S BRIDE

Three Summers since I chose a maid,
Too young maybe – but more's to do
At harvest-time than bide and woo.
    When us was wed she turned afraid
Of love and me and all things human;
Like the shut of a winter's day.
Her smile went out, and 'twasn't a woman –
    More like a little frightened fay.
        One night, in the Fall, she runned away.

    'Out 'mong the sheep, her be,' they said,
    'Should properly have been abed;
    But sure enough she wasn't there
    Lying awake with her wide brown stare.
So over seven-acre field and up-along across the down
    We chased her, flying like a hare

Before our lanterns. To Church-Town
    All in a shiver and a scare
We caught her, fetched her home at last
    And turned the key upon her, fast.

She does the work about the house
As well as most, but like a mouse:
    Happy enough to chat and play
    With birds and rabbits and such as they,
    So long as men-folk keep away.
'Not near, not near!' her eyes beseech
When one of us comes within reach.
    The women say that beasts in stall
    Look round like children at her call.
    I've hardly heard her speak at all.

Shy as a leveret, swift as he,
Straight and slight as a young larch tree,
Sweet as the first wild violets, she,
To her wild self. But what to me?

The short days shorten and the oaks are brown.
    The blue smoke rises to the low grey sky,
One leaf in the still air falls slowly down,
    A magpie's spotted feathers lie
On the black earth spread white with rime,
The berries redden up to Christmas-time.
    What's Christmas-time without there be
    Some other in the house than we!

    She sleeps up in the attic there
    Alone, poor maid. 'Tis but a stair
Betwixt us. Oh! my God! The down,
    The soft young down of her, the brown,
The brown of her – her eyes, her hair, her hair!

57

OSCAR WILDE
(1854–1900)

In 1895 Oscar Wilde was sentenced to two years' imprisonment with hard labour for 'gross indecency'. During his imprisonment a trooper in the Royal Horse Guards, Charles Wooldridge, was hanged for cutting his wife's throat. Wilde wrote *The Ballad of Reading Gaol* after his release. These are the first 10 stanzas:

He did not wear his scarlet coat,
    For blood and wine are red,
And blood and wine were on his hands
    When they found him with the dead,
The poor dead woman whom he loved,
    And murdered in her bed.

He walked amongst the Trial Men
    In a suit of shabby gray;
A cricket cap was on his head,
    And his step seemed light and gay;
But I never saw a man who looked
    So wistfully at the day.

I never saw a man who looked
    With such a wistful eye
Upon that little tent of blue
    Which prisoners call the sky,

And at every drifting cloud that went
    With sails of silver by.

I walked with other souls in pain,
    Within another ring,
And was wondering if the man had done
    A great or little thing,
When a voice behind me whispered low,
    'That fellow's got to swing.'

Dear Christ! the very prison walls
    Suddenly seemed to reel,
And the sky above my head became
    Like a casque of scorching steel;
And, though I was a soul in pain,
    My pain I could not feel.

I only knew what hunted thought
    Quickened his step, and why
He looked upon the garish day
    With such a wistful eye;
The man had killed the thing he loved,
    And so he had to die.

Yet each man kills the thing he loves,
    By each let this be heard,
Some do it with a bitter look,
    Some with a flattering word,
The coward does it with a kiss,
    The brave man with a sword!

Some kill their love when they are young,
    And some when they are old;
Some strangle with the hands of Lust,
    Some with the hands of Gold:

The kindest use a knife, because
    The dead so soon grow cold.

Some love too little, some too long,
    Some sell, and others buy;
Some do the deed with many tears,
    And some without a sigh:
For each man kills the thing he loves,
    Yet each man does not die.

He does not die a death of shame
    On a day of dark disgrace,
Nor have a noose about his neck,
    Nor a cloth upon his face,
Nor drop feet foremost through the floor
    Into an empty space.

58

ALGERNON CHARLES SWINBURNE
(1837–1909)

Algernon Charles Swinburne is usually regarded as the foremost of the English 'decadent' poets. Published in *Poems and Ballads* (1866), 'The Leper' helped to enhance his scandalous reputation. The story is told by a scribe who loved a beautiful, high-born woman. But she scorned him – 'A poor scribe, nowise great or fair' – and was herself in love with a knight. Though hopeless, the scribe pines away with desire:

> I served her in a royal house;
> > I served her wine and curious meat.
> For will to kiss between her brows,
> > I had no heart to sleep or eat.

However, the woman contracts leprosy:

> God, that makes time and ruins it
> > And alters not, abiding God,
> Changed with disease her body sweet,
> > The body of love wherein she abode.

The scribe still loves her, but she is vilified and driven out:

> Love is more sweet and comelier
> > Than a dove's throat strained out to sing.
> All they spat out and cursed at her
> > And cast her forth for a base thing.

They cursed her, seeing how God had wrought
    This curse to plague her, a curse of his.
Fools were they surely, seeing not
    How sweeter than all sweet she is.

The knight, too, shuns her:

Yea, he inside whose grasp all night
    Her fervent body leapt or lay,
Stained with sharp kisses red and white,
    Found her a plague to spurn away.

But the scribe takes her in:

I hid her in this wattled house,
    I served her water and poor bread.
For joy to kiss between her brows
    Time upon time I was nigh dead.

Bread failed; we got but well-water
    And gathered grass with dropping seed.
I had such joy of kissing her,
    I had small care to sleep or feed.

The woman dies, but six months later the scribe still cherishes her dead
body:

Six months, and I sit still and hold
    In two cold palms her cold two feet.
Her hair, half grey half ruined gold,
    Thrills me and burns me in kissing it.

Love bites and stings me through, to see
    Her keen face made of sunken bones.
Her worn-off eyelids madden me,
    That were shot through with purple once.

Necrophilia is clearly suggested, an aberration not otherwise present in Swinburne's stock of deviant practices.

He was wildly popular among the aesthetic young for his sweeping metaphysical grandeur, as in the Chorus of *Atalanta in Calydon*:

> Before the beginning of years
> There came to the making of man
> Time, with a gift of tears;
> Grief, with a glass that ran;
> Pleasure, with pain for leaven;
> Summer, with flowers that fell;
> Remembrance fallen from heaven,
> And madness risen from hell;
> Strength without hands to smite,
> Love that endures for a breath:
> Night, the shadow of light,
> And life, the shadow of death.

59

THOMAS HARDY
(1840–1928)

Thomas Hardy was, unusually, a great novelist as well as a great poet. Some of his poems, such as 'In the Study', show a novelist's keen social observation. Ezra Pound said that the poem was the fruit of having written 20 novels first.

IN THE STUDY

He enters, and mute on the edge of a chair
Sits a thin-faced lady, a stranger there,
A type of decayed gentility;
And by some small signs he well can guess
That she comes to him almost breakfastless.

'I have called – I hope I do not err –
I am looking for a purchaser
Of some score volumes of the works
Of eminent divines I own, –
Left by my father – though it irks
My patience to offer them.' And she smiles
As if necessity were unknown;
'But the truth of it is that oftenwhiles
I have wished, as I am fond of art,
To make my rooms a little smart,
And these old books are so in the way.'

And lightly still she laughs to him,
As if to sell were a mere gay whim,
And that, to be frank, Life were indeed
To her not vinegar and gall,
But fresh and honey-like; and Need
No household skeleton at all.

Hardy's early religious beliefs seem to have ebbed over the years and
been replaced by belief in an impersonal and perhaps malign force
which he calls, at the end of *Tess of the d'Urbervilles* (1891), 'the
President of the Immortals'. In one of his most famous poems, 'The
Darkling Thrush', written in December 1900, the bird's joyful song
seems to reflect something he cannot share.

THE DARKLING THRUSH

I leant upon a coppice gate
    When Frost was spectre-gray,
And Winter's dregs made desolate
    The weakening eye of day.
The tangled bine-stems scored the sky
    Like strings of broken lyres,
And all mankind that haunted nigh
    Had sought their household fires.

The land's sharp features seemed to be
    The Century's corpse outleant,
His crypt the cloudy canopy,
    The wind his death-lament.
The ancient pulse of germ and birth
    Was shrunken hard and dry,
And every spirit upon earth
    Seemed fervourless as I.

At once a voice arose among
    The bleak twigs overhead

In a full-hearted evensong
    Of joy illimited;
An aged thrush, frail, gaunt, and small,
    In blast-beruffled plume,
Had chosen thus to fling his soul
    Upon the growing gloom.

So little cause for carolings
    Of such ecstatic sound
Was written on terrestrial things
    Afar or nigh around,
That I could think there trembled through
    His happy good-night air
Some blessed Hope, whereof he knew
    And I was unaware.

In 'The Oxen', written after the outbreak of the First World War, the inability to believe and the wish to believe seem to co-exist.

THE OXEN

Christmas Eve, and twelve of the clock.
    'Now they are all on their knees,'
An elder said as we sat in a flock
    By the embers in hearthside ease.

We pictured the meek mild creatures where
    They dwelt in their strawy pen,
Nor did it occur to one of us there
    To doubt they were kneeling then.

So fair a fancy few would weave
    In these years! Yet, I feel,
If someone said on Christmas Eve,
    'Come; see the oxen kneel

'In the lonely barton by yonder coomb
    Our childhood used to know,'
I should go with him in the gloom,
        Hoping it might be so.

Hardy's marriage to Emma Gifford had not been happy, but his most poignant poems are those in which he remembers her after her death in 1912. By the time she died they slept in separate rooms, and in 'The Going' he reproaches her for dying without warning. It was written in 1912.

THE GOING

Why did you give no hint that night
That quickly after the morrow's dawn,
And calmly, as if indifferent quite,
You would close your term here, up and be gone
        Where I could not follow
        With wing of swallow
To gain one glimpse of you ever anon!

        Never to bid good-bye,
        Or lip me the softest call,
Or utter a wish for a word, while I
Saw morning harden upon the wall,
        Unmoved, unknowing
        That your great going
Had place that moment, and altered all.

Why do you make me leave the house
And think for a breath it is you I see
At the end of the alley of bending boughs
Where so often at dusk you used to be;
        Till in darkening dankness
        The yawning blankness
Of the perspective sickens me!

You were she who abode
By those red-veined rocks far West,
You were the swan-necked one who rode
Along the beetling Beeny Crest,
    And, reining nigh me,
    Would muse and eye me,
While Life unrolled us its very best.

Why, then, latterly did we not speak,
Did we not think of those days long dead,
And ere your vanishing strive to seek
That time's renewal? We might have said,
    'In this bright spring weather
    We'll visit together
Those places that once we visited.'

    Well, well! All's past amend,
    Unchangeable. It must go.
I seem but a dead man held on end
To sink down soon. . . . O you could not know
    That such swift fleeing
    No soul foreseeing –
Not even I – would undo me so!

60

RUDYARD KIPLING
(1865–1936)

Rudyard Kipling is known as an imperialist, but he had a keen sense of how transient empires are:

> Cities and Thrones and Powers
> > Stand in Time's eye,
> Almost as long as flowers,
> > Which daily die . . .

In his historical fantasy *Puck of Pook's Hill*, that song is sung by a Roman centurion stationed in Britain. But Kipling knew that the British empire would vanish as the Roman had, and said so in his poem 'Recessional', written in 1887 for Queen Victoria's Golden Jubilee, 'Lo, all our pomp of yesterday / Is one with Nineveh and Tyre'. In 'The Way through the Woods' he delights in the thought of nature (and ghosts) reclaiming the land.

THE WAY THROUGH THE WOODS

They shut the road through the woods
Seventy years ago.
Weather and rain have undone it again,
And now you would never know
There was once a road through the woods
Before they planted the trees.

It is underneath the coppice and heath
And the thin anemones.
Only the keeper sees
That, where the ring-dove broods,
And the badgers roll at ease,
There was once a road through the woods.

Yet, if you enter the woods
Of a summer evening late,
When the night-air cools on the trout-ringed pools
Where the otter whistles his mate,
(They fear not men in the woods,
Because they see so few)
You will hear the beat of a horse's feet,
And the swish of a skirt in the dew,
Steadily cantering through
The misty solitudes,
As though they perfectly knew
The old lost road through the woods . . .
But there is no road through the woods.

61

A.E. HOUSMAN
(1859–1936)

Alfred Edward Housman was gay, and he thought it unjust that he should be made to feel guilty about something that was part of his nature. To make matters worse, he fell in love at Oxford with a hetero-sexual oarsman, who rebuffed him. Housman did not know, he wrote, 'Whatever brute and blackguard made the world', but it cannot be the just God that Christians believe in.

Oscar Wilde's imprisonment prompted him to write 'Oh who is that young sinner', and his brother Laurence courageously published it in 1936, after Housman's death.

OH WHO IS THAT YOUNG SINNER

Oh who is that young sinner with the handcuffs on his wrists?
And what has he been after that they groan and shake their fists?
And wherefore is he wearing such a conscience-stricken air?
Oh they're taking him to prison for the colour of his hair.

'Tis a shame to human nature, such a head of hair as his;
In the good old time 'twas hanging for the colour that it is;
Though hanging isn't bad enough, and flaying would be fair
For the nameless and abominable colour of his hair.

Oh a deal of pains he's taken and a pretty price he's paid
To hide his poll or dye it of a mentionable shade;

But they've pulled the beggar's hat off for the world to see and
    stare,
And they're haling him to justice for the colour of his hair.

Now 'tis oakum for his fingers and the treadmill for his feet
And the quarry-gang on Portland in the cold and in the heat,
And between his spells of labour in the time he has to spare
He can curse the God that made him for the colour of his hair.

A more personal treatment of the same subject is 'Because I liked you
better':

BECAUSE I LIKED YOU BETTER

Because I liked you better
    Than suits a man to say,
It irked you, and I promised
    To throw the thought away.

To put the world between us
    We parted, stiff and dry;
'Good-bye,' said you, 'forget me.'
    'I will, no fear,' said I.

If here, where clover whitens
    The dead man's knoll, you pass,
And no tall flower to meet you
    Starts in the trefoiled grass,

Halt by the headstone naming
    The heart you have not stirred,
And say the lad that loved you
    Was one that kept his word.

Housman's bitterness extends to his nature poetry, in that he knows his
love of nature is not reciprocated:

TELL ME NOT HERE, IT NEEDS NOT SAYING

Tell me not here, it needs not saying,
        What tune the enchantress plays
In aftermaths of soft September
        Or under blanching mays,
For she and I were long acquainted
        And I knew all her ways.

On russet floors, by waters idle,
        The pine lets fall its cone;
The cuckoo shouts all day at nothing
        In leafy dells alone;
And traveller's joy beguiles in autumn
        Hearts that have lost their own.

On acres of the seeded grasses
        The changing burnish heaves;
Or marshalled under moons of harvest
        Stand still all night the sheaves;
Or beeches strip in storms for winter
        And stain the wind with leaves.

Possess, as I possessed a season,
        The countries I resign,
Where over elmy plains the highway
        Would mount the hills and shine,
And full of shade the pillared forest
        Would murmur and be mine.

For nature, heartless, witless nature,
        Will neither care nor know
What stranger's feet may find the meadow
        And trespass there and go,
Nor ask amid the dews of morning
        If they are mine or no.

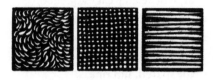

62

GERARD MANLEY HOPKINS
(1844–89)

In Hopkins's poetry nature is the expression of God's glory, and sometimes of his terror. 'Spring and Fall: to a young child' teaches the integration of the human and the natural.

SPRING AND FALL: TO A YOUNG CHILD

Márgarét, áre you grieving
Over Goldengrove unleaving?
Leáves, like the things of man, you
With your fresh thoughts care for, can you?
Áh! ás the heart grows older
It will come to such sights colder
By and by, nor spare a sigh
Though worlds of wanwood leafmeal lie;
And yet you will weep and know why.
Now no matter, child, the name:
Sórrow's springs áre the same.
Nor mouth had, no nor mind, expressed
What heart heard of, ghost guessed:
It is the blight man was born for,
It is Margaret you mourn for.

'Binsey Poplars, felled 1879', especially apposite today, mourns human destructiveness. Binsey is a village near Oxford.

BINSEY POPLARS, FELLED 1879

My aspens dear, whose airy cages quelled,
Quelled or quenched in leaves the leaping sun,
All felled, felled, are all felled;
    Of a fresh and following folded rank
         Not spared, not one
         That dandled a sandalled
    Shadow that swam or sank
On meadow and river and wind-wandering weed-
    winding bank.

O if we but knew what we do
         When we delve or hew –
    Hack and rack the growing green!
         Since country is so tender
    To touch, her being sò slender,
    That, like this sleek and seeing ball
    But a prick will make no eye at all,
    Where we, even where we mean
         To mend her we end her,
         When we hew or delve:
After-comers cannot guess the beauty been.
    Ten or twelve, only ten or twelve
         Strokes of havoc unselve
            The sweet especial scene,
         Rural scene, a rural scene,
         Sweet especial rural scene.

63

EDWARD THOMAS
(1878–1917)

Edward Thomas has a distinctive poetic voice, gentle, regretful, elusive.
'Old Man' illustrates it well. The plant the poem refers to has many
names, including 'old man' and 'lad's love'. It is a bush with grey-green
leaves and a strong camphor-like smell. The child in the poem is
Thomas's younger daughter, Myfanwy.

OLD MAN

Old Man, or Lad's-love, – in the name there's nothing
To one that knows not Lad's-love, or Old Man,
The hoar-green feathery herb, almost a tree,
Growing with rosemary and lavender.
Even to one that knows it well, the names
Half decorate, half perplex, the thing it is:
At least, what that is clings not to the names
In spite of time. And yet I like the names.

The herb itself I like not, but for certain
I love it, as some day the child will love it
Who plucks a feather from the door-side bush
Whenever she goes in or out of the house.
Often she waits there, snipping the tips and shrivelling
The shreds at last on to the path, perhaps
Thinking, perhaps of nothing, till she sniffs

Her fingers and runs off. The bush is still
But half as tall as she, though it is as old;
So well she clips it. Not a word she says;
And I can only wonder how much hereafter
She will remember, with that bitter scent,
Of garden rows, and ancient damson trees
Topping a hedge, a bent path to a door,
A low thick bush beside the door, and me
Forbidding her to pick.
      As for myself,
Where first I met the bitter scent is lost.
I, too, often shrivel the grey shreds,
Sniff them and think and sniff again and try
Once more to think what it is I am remembering,
Always in vain. I cannot like the scent,
Yet I would rather give up others more sweet,
With no meaning, than this bitter one.
I have mislaid the key. I sniff the spray
And think of nothing; I see and I hear nothing;
Yet seem, too, to be listening, lying in wait
For what I should, yet never can, remember;
No garden appears, no path, no hoar-green bush
Of Lad's-love or Old Man, no child beside,
Neither father nor mother, nor any playmate;
Only an avenue, dark, nameless, without end.

Thomas was not an easy man to live with, as can be gathered from the memoir published by his widow, Helen. That he realised this can be gathered from the next poem.

AND YOU, HELEN

And you, Helen, what should I give you?
So many things I would give you
Had I an infinite great store
Offered me and I stood before

To choose. I would give you youth,
All kinds of loveliness and truth,
A clear eye as good as mine,
Lands, waters, flowers, wine,
As many children as your heart
Might wish for, a far better art
Than mine can be, all you have lost
Upon the travelling waters tossed,
Or given to me. If I could choose
Freely in that great treasure-house
Anything from any shelf,
I would give you back yourself,
And power to discriminate
What you want and want it not too late,
Many fair days free from care
And heart to enjoy both foul and fair,
And myself, too, if I could find
Where it lay hidden and it proved kind.

64

ROBERT FROST
(1874–1963)

Robert Frost's poem 'Out, Out' is about a 16-year-old boy he knew in New Hampshire who bled to death when his hand was accidentally cut off by a buzz-saw. The title is from Shakespeare's *Macbeth* ('Out, out, brief candle').

OUT, OUT

The buzz-saw snarled and rattled in the yard
And made dust and dropped stove-length sticks of wood,
Sweet-scented stuff when the breeze drew across it.
And from there those that lifted eyes could count
Five mountain ranges one behind the other
Under the sunset far into Vermont.
And the saw snarled and rattled, snarled and rattled,
As it ran light, or had to bear a load.
And nothing happened: day was all but done.
Call it a day, I wish they might have said
To please the boy by giving him the half hour
That a boy counts so much when saved from work.
His sister stood beside them in her apron
To tell them 'Supper'. At the word, the saw,
As if to prove saws knew what supper meant,
Leaped out at the boy's hand, or seemed to leap –
He must have given the hand. However it was,

Neither refused the meeting. But the hand!
The boy's first outcry was a rueful laugh,
As he swung toward them holding up the hand
Half in appeal, but half as if to keep
The life from spilling. Then the boy saw all –
Since he was old enough to know, big boy
Doing a man's work, though a child at heart –
He saw all spoiled. 'Don't let him cut my hand off –
The doctor, when he comes. Don't let him, sister!'
So. But the hand was gone already.
The doctor put him in the dark of ether.
He lay and puffed his lips out with his breath.
And then – the watcher at his pulse took fright.
No one believed. They listened at his heart,
Little – less – nothing! – and that ended it.
No more to build on there. And they, since they
Were not the one dead, turned to their affairs.

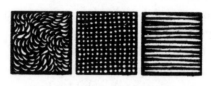

65

W.H. DAVIES
(1870–1940)

W.H. Davies was a Welsh poet who spent much of his life as a tramp or hobo in Britain and North America. The *Autobiography of a Super-Tramp* (1908) describes his American adventures. He was drawn to Canada by news of the Klondike Gold Rush, and suffered a life-changing accident in 1899. Attempting to jump a freight train in Ontario, he fell, and as a result one leg had to be amputated below the knee. He wore a wooden leg for the rest of his life.

As a poet he drew the attention of many English literary figures, including D.H. Lawrence, George Bernard Shaw, the Sitwells and Edward Thomas, who rented a cottage for him near his own. His most famous poem is 'Leisure', which opens:

> What is this life if full of care,
> We have no time to stand and stare? . . .

But more remarkable is 'The Sleepers'.

THE SLEEPERS

> As I walked down the waterside
> This silent morning, wet and dark;
> Before the cocks in farmyards crowed,
> Before the dogs began to bark;
> Before the hour of five was struck
> By old Westminster's mighty clock:

As I walked down the waterside
This morning, in the cold damp air,
I saw a hundred women and men
Huddled in rags and sleeping there:
These people have no work, thought I,
And long before their time they die.

That moment, on the waterside,
A lighted car came at a bound;
I looked inside, and saw a score
Of pale and weary men that frowned;
Each man sat in a huddled heap,
Carried to work while fast asleep.

Ten cars rushed down the waterside
Like lighted coffins in the dark;
With twenty dead men in each car,
That must be brought alive by work:
These people work too hard, thought I,
And long before their time they die.

Another poem that it is hard to forget is 'The Inquest'.

THE INQUEST

I took my oath I would inquire,
    Without affection, hate, or wrath,
Into the death of Ada Wright –
    So help me God! I took that oath.

When I went out to see the corpse,
    The four months' babe that died so young,
I judged it was seven pounds in weight,
    And little more than one foot long.

One eye, that had a yellow lid,
  Was shut – so was the mouth, that smiled;
The left eye open, shining bright –
  It seemed a knowing little child.

For as I looked at that one eye,
  It seemed to laugh, and say with glee:
'What caused my death you'll never know –
  Perhaps my mother murdered me.'

When I went into court again,
  To hear the mother's evidence –
It was a love-child, she explained.
  And smiled, for our intelligence.

'Now, Gentlemen of the Jury,' said
  The coroner – 'this woman's child
By misadventure met its death.'
  'Aye, aye,' said we. The mother smiled.

And I could see that child's one eye
  Which seemed to laugh, and say with glee:
'What caused my death you'll never know –
  Perhaps my mother murdered me.'

66

G.K. CHESTERTON
(1874–1936)

G.K. Chesterton was a master of paradox, which he defined as 'Truth standing on its head to attract attention'. He was a Christian, and saw Christianity as essentially a paradoxical religion, in that its idea of triumph is a criminal hanging on a cross between two other criminals. This view of Christianity drew him to celebrate unspectacular, unassuming beings. By contrast with Conan Doyle's dramatic Sherlock Holmes, his detective, Father Brown, is a stumpy Catholic priest with shapeless clothes and a large umbrella. Chesterton's poem, 'The Donkey', makes the same point.

THE DONKEY

When fishes flew and forests walked
    And figs grew upon thorn,
Some moment when the moon was blood
    Then surely I was born.

With monstrous head and sickening cry
    And ears like errant wings
The devil's walking parody
    On all four-footed things.

The tattered outlaw of the earth,
    Of ancient crooked will;

Starve, scourge, deride me: I am dumb,
   I keep my secret still.

Fools! For I also had my hour;
   One far fierce hour and sweet:
There was a shout about my ears,
   And palms before my feet.

Typically, in Chesterton's poetic masterpiece 'Lepanto', the hero, Don John of Austria, is presented as somehow sub-standard – 'crownless', 'half-attainted', a 'troubadour'. This is a slight distortion of history. While it is true that Don John was illegitimate, the son of Holy Roman Emperor Charles V and a singer, his noble status was never in question. He was appointed by his half-brother, Philip II of Spain, to command the fleet of the Holy League, an alliance of Catholic states arranged by Pope Pius V. The 'enormous silence', followed by the 'tiny' noise of the Crusade, recalls, perhaps deliberately, I Kings 19:11–12, where, after a mighty wind, an earthquake and a fire, God comes to Elijah as a 'still, small voice' – a very Chestertonian touch.

   The Holy League won a spectacular victory at the Battle of Lepanto, 1571, destroying the entire Turkish fleet. Tourists can still be taken by boat to see, through the shallow water of the Gulf of Corinth, the remains of the Turkish fleet on the seabed. It was the last great naval battle in which the ships on both sides were rowing vessels, descendants of the ancient triremes, manned largely by slaves and captives. Cervantes, the author of *Don Quixote,* who makes an appearance at the poem's end, really did fight at Lepanto, serving with the Spanish contingent of the Holy League fleet.

LEPANTO

White founts falling in the courts of the sun,
And the Soldan of Byzantium is smiling as they run;
There is laughter like the fountains in that face of all men feared,
It stirs the forest darkness, the darkness of his beard,
It curls the blood-red crescent, the crescent of his lips,

For the inmost sea of all the earth is shaken with his ships.
They have dared the white republics up the capes of Italy,
They have dashed the Adriatic round the Lion of the Sea,
And the Pope has cast his arms abroad for agony and loss,
And called the kings of Christendom for swords about the Cross,
The cold queen of England is looking in the glass;
The shadow of the Valois is yawning at the Mass;
From evening isles fantastical rings faint the Spanish gun,
And the Lord upon the Golden Horn is laughing in the sun.

Dim drums throbbing, in the hills half heard,
Where only on a nameless throne a crownless prince has stirred,
Where, risen from a doubtful seat and half-attainted stall,
The last Knight of Europe takes weapons from the wall,
The last and lingering troubadour to whom the bird has sung,
That once went singing southward when all the world was young,
In that enormous silence, tiny and unafraid,
Comes up along a winding road the noise of the Crusade.
Strong gongs groaning as the guns boom far,
Don John of Austria is going to the war,
Stiff flags straining in the night-blasts cold
In the gloom black-purple, in the glint old-gold,
Torchlight crimson on the copper kettle-drums,
Then the tuckets, then the trumpets, then the cannon, and he
    comes.
Don John laughing in the brave beard curled,
Spurning of his stirrups like the thrones of all the world,
Holding his head up for a flag of all the free.
Love-light of Spain – hurrah!
Death-light of Africa!
Don John of Austria
Is riding to the sea . . .

King Philip's in his closet with the Fleece about his neck
(Don John of Austria is armed upon the deck.)
The walls are hung with velvet that is black and soft as sin,

And little dwarfs creep out of it and little dwarfs creep in.
He holds a crystal phial that has colours like the moon,
He touches, and it tingles, and he trembles very soon,
And his face is as a fungus of a leprous white and grey
Like plants in the high houses that are shuttered from the day,
And death is in the phial, and the end of noble work,
But Don John of Austria has fired upon the Turk.
Don John's hunting, and his hounds have bayed –
Booms away past Italy the rumour of his raid.
Gun upon gun, ha! ha!
Gun upon gun, hurrah!
Don John of Austria
Has loosed the cannonade.

The Pope was in his chapel before day or battle broke,
(Don John of Austria is hidden in the smoke.)
The hidden room in a man's house where God sits all the year,
The secret window whence the world looks small and very dear.
He sees as in a mirror on the monstrous twilight sea
The crescent of his cruel ships whose name is mystery;
They fling great shadows foe-wards, making Cross and Castle dark,
They veil the plumèd lions on the galleys of St. Mark;
And above the ships are palaces of brown, black-bearded chiefs,
And below the ships are prisons, where with multitudinous griefs,
Christian captives sick and sunless, all a labouring race repines
Like a race in sunken cities, like a nation in the mines.
They are lost like slaves that swat, and in the skies of morning hung
The stairways of the tallest gods when tyranny was young.

They are countless, voiceless, hopeless as those fallen or fleeing on
Before the high Kings' horses in the granite of Babylon.
And many a one grows witless in his quiet room in hell
Where a yellow face looks inward through the lattice of his cell,
And he finds his God forgotten, and he seeks no more a sign –
(But Don John of Austria has burst the battle-line!)
Don John pounding from the slaughter-painted poop,

Purpling all the ocean like a bloody pirate's sloop,
Scarlet running over on the silvers and the golds,
Breaking of the hatches up and bursting of the holds,
Thronging of the thousands up that labour under sea
White for bliss and blind for sun and stunned for liberty.
Vivat Hispania!
Domino Gloria!
Don John of Austria
Has set his people free.

Cervantes on his galley sets the sword back in the sheath
(Don John of Austria rides homeward with a wreath.)
And he sees across a weary land a straggling road in Spain,
Up which a lean and foolish knight for ever rides in vain,
And he smiles, but not as Sultans smile, and settles back the
    blade . . .
(But Don John of Austria rides home from the Crusade.)

67

ROBERT GRAVES
(1895–1985)

Robert Graves, as well as being a poet and novelist, was a pioneering literary critic, particularly in his collaboration with Laura Riding, with whom he wrote *A Survey of Modernist Poetry* (1927, the same year in which 'The Cool Web', below, was first published). Their ideas about poetic ambiguity prefigured William Empson's *Seven Types of Ambiguity* (1930).

THE COOL WEB

Children are dumb to say how hot the day is,
How hot the scent is of the summer rose,
How dreadful the black wastes of evening sky,
How dreadful the tall soldiers drumming by.

But we have speech, to chill the angry day,
And speech, to dull the rose's cruel scent.
We spell away the overhanging night,
We spell away the soldiers and the fright.

There's a cool web of language winds us in,
Retreat from too much joy or too much fear:
We grow sea-green at last and coldly die
In brininess and volubility.

But if we let our tongues lose self-possession,
Throwing off language and its watery clasp
Before our death, instead of when death comes,
Facing the wide glare of the children's day,
Facing the rose, the dark sky and the drums,
We shall go mad no doubt and die that way.

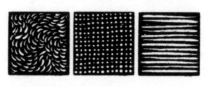

68

D.H. LAWRENCE
(1885–1930)

For many readers, D.H. Lawrence was an even greater poet than he was a novelist. The subjects of his poems span the whole of his life. In 'Piano' he remembers musical evenings in his childhood home, when he would crouch under the piano while his mother played. In 'Bavarian Gentians' he imagines the blue flowers as torches that will light his way into Pluto's underground realm of death. For me, though, his greatest poem is 'Snake', which recalls an incident in Taormina, Sicily, and touches on some of Lawrence's deepest beliefs.

SNAKE

A snake came to my water-trough
On a hot, hot day, and I in pyjamas for the heat,
To drink there.

In the deep, strange-scented shade of the great dark
        carob-tree
I came down the steps with my pitcher
And must wait, must stand and wait, for there he was
        at the trough before me.

He reached down from a fissure in the earth-wall in
        the gloom

And trailed his yellow-brown slackness soft-bellied down,
    over the edge of the stone trough
And rested his throat upon the stone bottom,
And where the water had dripped from the tap, in a
    small clearness,
He sipped with his straight mouth,
Softly drank through his straight gums, into his slack
    long body,
Silently.

Someone was before me at my water-trough,
And I, like a second-comer, waiting.
He lifted his head from his drinking, as cattle do,
And looked at me vaguely, as drinking cattle do,
And flickered his two-forked tongue from his lips, and
    mused a moment,
And stooped and drank a little more,
Being earth-brown, earth-golden from the burning bowels
    of the earth
On the day of Sicilian July, with Etna smoking.

The voice of my education said to me
He must be killed,
For in Sicily the black, black snakes are innocent, the
    gold are venomous.

And voices in me said, If you were a man
You would take a stick and break him now, and finish
    him off.

But must I confess how I liked him,
How glad I was he had come like a guest in quiet, to
    drink at my water-trough
And depart peaceful, pacified, and thankless,
Into the burning bowels of this earth?

Was it cowardice, that I dared not kill him?
Was it perversity, that I longed to talk to him?
Was it humility, to feel so honoured?
I felt so honoured.

And yet those voices:
If you were not afraid, you would kill him!

And truly I was afraid, I was most afraid,
But even so, honoured still more
That he should seek my hospitality
From out the dark door of the secret earth.

He drank enough
And lifted his head, dreamily, as one who has drunken,
And flickered his tongue like a forked night on the air,
      so black,
Seeming to lick his lips,
And looked around like a god, unseeing, into the air,
And slowly turned his head,
And slowly, very slowly, as if thrice adream,
Proceeded to draw his slow length curving round
And climb again the broken bank of my wall-face.

And as he put his head into that dreadful hole,
As he slowly drew up, snake-easing his shoulders,
      and entered farther,
A sort of horror, a sort of protest against his withdrawing
      into that horrid black hole,
Deliberately going into the blackness, and slowly drawing
      himself after,
Overcame me now his back was turned.

I looked round, I put down my pitcher,
I picked up a clumsy log
And threw it at the water-trough with a clatter.

I think it did not hit him,
But suddenly that part of him that was left behind
    convulsed in undignified haste,
Writhed like lightning, and was gone
Into the black hole, the earth-tipped fissure in the wall-front,
At which, in the intense still noon, I stared with fascination.

And immediately I regretted it.
I thought how paltry, how vulgar, what a mean act!
I despised myself and the voices of my accursed human education.

And I thought of the albatross,
And I wished he would come back, my snake.

For he seemed to me again like a king,
Like a king in exile, uncrowned in the underworld,
Now due to be crowned again.

And so, I missed my chance with one of the lords
Of life.
And I have something to expiate;
A pettiness.

69

WILFRED OWEN
(1893 – 1918)

Shortly before he was killed Wilfred Owen wrote a Preface to his as-then unpublished poems, which states:

My subject is War, and the pity of War.
The Poetry is in the pity.

'Disabled' illustrates this.

DISABLED

He sat in a wheeled chair, waiting for dark,
And shivered in his ghastly suit of grey,
Legless, sewn short at elbow. Through the park
Voices of boys rang saddening like a hymn,
Voices of play and pleasure after day,
Till gathering sleep had mothered them from him.

About this time Town used to swing so gay
When glow-lamps budded in the light blue trees,
And girls glanced lovelier as the air grew dim, –
In the old times, before he threw away his knees.
Now he will never feel again how slim
Girls' waists are, or how warm their subtle hands.
All of them touch him like some queer disease.

There was an artist silly for his face,
For it was younger than his youth, last year.
Now, he is old; his back will never brace;
He's lost his colour very far from here,
Poured it down shell-holes till the veins ran dry,
And half his lifetime lapsed in the hot race
And leap of purple spurted from his thigh.

One time he liked a blood-smear down his leg,
After the matches, carried shoulder-high.
It was after football, when he'd drunk a peg,
He thought he'd better join. – He wonders why.
Someone had said he'd look a god in kilts,
That's why; and maybe, too, to please his Meg;
Aye, that was it, to please the giddy jilts
He asked to join. He didn't have to beg;
Smiling they wrote his lie: aged nineteen years.

Germans he scarcely thought of, all their guilt,
And Austria's, did not move him. And no fears
Of Fear came yet. He thought of jewelled hilts
For daggers in plaid socks; of smart salutes;
And care of arms; and leave; and pay arrears;
Esprit de corps; and hints for young recruits.
And soon, he was drafted out with drums and cheers.

Some cheered him home, but not as crowds cheer Goal.
Only a solemn man who brought him fruits
Thanked him; and then enquired about his soul.

Now, he will spend a few sick years in institutes,
And do what things the rules consider wise,
And take whatever pity they may dole.
Tonight he noticed how the women's eyes
Passed from him to the strong men that were whole.
How cold and late it is! Why don't they come
And get him into bed? Why don't they come?

70

ISAAC ROSENBERG
(1890–1918)

Isaac Rosenberg was the son of poor Lithuanian Jewish immigrants living in London's East End. A gifted artist, he was apprenticed to an engraver for a time, but raised funds to attend the Slade School of Fine Art, where his fellow students included Stanley Spencer. He exhibited paintings at the Whitechapel Gallery in 1914. That same year he joined his sister Mina in Cape Town, hoping the climate would ease his chronic bronchitis. 'Nothing can justify war,' he wrote, adding, 'I suppose we must all fight to get this trouble over.' So he returned to England and enlisted in 1915, joining a 'Bantam battalion', for men under the usual minimum height of 5 foot 3 inches, and arranged that half his pay should be sent to his mother. He was killed on 1 April 1918. His self-portrait hangs in the National Portrait Gallery.

This poem is unusual among his war poems in recording a moment of joy.

RETURNING, WE HEAR THE LARKS

Sombre the night is.
And though we have our lives, we know
What sinister threat lurks there.

Dragging these anguished limbs, we only know
This poison-blasted track opens on our camp –
On a little safe sleep.

But hark! joy – joy – strange joy.
Lo! heights of night ringing with unseen larks.
Music showering on our upturned list'ning faces.

Death could drop from the dark
As easily as song –
But song only dropped,
Like a blind man's dreams on the sand
By dangerous tides,
Like a girl's dark hair for she dreams no ruin lies there,
Or her kisses where a serpent hides.

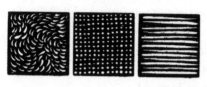

71

MAY WEDDERBURN CANNAN
(1893–1973)

At 21, May Wedderburn Cannan, daughter of the dean of Trinity College, Oxford, volunteered for four weeks at The Coffee Shop, a railway canteen for soldiers in Rouen. She did not, in fact, belong to a Voluntary Aid Detachment (VAD) nursing unit in France, but Philip Larkin, choosing 'Rouen' for his *Oxford Book of Twentieth-Century Verse* (1973), commented, 'it has all the warmth and idealism of the VADs in the First World War. I find it enchanting.'

'Tatties' in the third stanza refers to the blinds or mats hung in a doorway or window.

ROUEN APRIL 26 – MAY 24 1915

Early morning over Rouen, hopeful, high, courageous morning,
And the laughter of adventure, and the steepness of the stair,
And the dawn across the river, and the wind across the bridges,
And the empty littered station, and the tired people there.

Can you recall those mornings, and the hurry of awakening,
And the long-forgotten wonder if we should miss the way,
And the unfamiliar faces, and the coming of provisions,
And the freshness and the glory of the labour of the day.

Hot noontide over Rouen, and the sun upon the city,
Sun and dust unceasing, and the glare of cloudless skies,

And the voices of the Indians and the endless stream of soldiers,
And the clicking of the tatties, and the buzzing of the flies.

Can you recall those noontides and the reek of steam and coffee,
Heavy-laden noontides with the evening's peace to win,
And the little piles of Woodbines, and the sticky soda bottles,
And the crushes in the 'Parlour', and the letters coming in?

Quiet night-time over Rouen, and the station full of soldiers,
All the youth and pride of England from the ends of all the earth;
And the rifles piled together, and the creaking of the sword-belts,
And the faces bent above them, and the gay, heart-breaking mirth.

Can I forget the passage from the cool white-bedded Aid Post
Past the long sun-blistered coaches of the khaki Red Cross train
To the truck train full of wounded, and the weariness and laughter
And 'Good-bye, and thank you, Sister', and the empty yards again?

Can you recall the parcels that we made them for the railroad,
Crammed and bulging parcels held together by their string,
And the voices of the sargeants who called the Drafts together,
And the agony and splendour when they stood to save the King?

Can you forget their passing, the cheering and the waving,
The little group of people at the doorway of the shed,
The sudden awful silence when the last train swung to darkness,
And the lonely desolation, and the mocking stars o'erhead?

Can you recall the midnights, and the footsteps of night watchers,
Men who came from darkness and went back to dark again,
And the shadows on the rail-lines and the all inglorious labour,
And the promise of the daylight firing blue the window-pane?

Can you recall the passing through the kitchen door to morning,
Morning very still and solemn breaking slowly on the town,
And the early coastways engines that had met the ships at daybreak,
And the Drafts just out from England, and the day shift coming down?

Can you forget returning slowly, stumbling on the cobbles,
And the white-decked Red Cross barges dropping seawards for the tide,
And the search for English papers, and the blessed cool, of water,
And the peace of half-closed shutters that shut out the world outside?

Can I forget the evenings and the sunsets on the island,
And the tall black ships at anchor far below our balcony,
And the distant call of bugles, and the white wine in the glasses,
And the long line of the street lamps, stretching Eastwards to the sea?

When the world slips slow to darkness, when the office fire burns lower,
My heart goes out to Rouen, Rouen all the world away;
When other men remember, I remember our Adventure
And the trains that go from Rouen at the ending of the day.

JOHN MCCRAE
(1872–1918)

John McCrae was a Canadian doctor. He served as a brigade medical officer, tending the wounded after the Second Battle of Ypres in 1915. His friend Lieutenant Alexis Helmer was killed in the battle, and his burial inspired this poem.

IN FLANDERS FIELDS

In Flanders fields the poppies blow
Between the crosses, row on row,
    That mark our place; and in the sky
    The larks, still bravely singing, fly
Scarce heard amid the guns below.

We are the Dead. Short days ago
We lived, felt dawn, saw sunset glow,
    Loved and were loved, and now we lie,
    In Flanders fields.

Take up our quarrel with the foe:
To you from failing hands we throw
    The torch; be yours to hold it high.
    If ye break faith with us who die
We shall not sleep, though poppies grow
    In Flanders fields.

W.B. YEATS
(1865–1939)

William Butler Yeats's wife, Georgie Hyde-Lees, discovered after their marriage in 1917 that she could contact spirit-guides while in a trance, and could record what they told her in unconscious ('automatic') writing. The spirits gave her an account of human history that divides it into periods of 2,000 years, with each period represented by two intersecting cones (or 'gyres'). They told her, too, that human beings undergo successive reincarnations after death. Much of Yeats's later poetry is based on these beliefs, and he published an account of them as *A Vision* in 1925.

'Leda and the Swan' is one of his greatest poems, and some readers may find its vividness disturbing. It was written in 1923, and in it Yeats sees the rape of Leda by Zeus, disguised as a swan, as ushering in the 2,000-year period of Greek civilisation, including the fall of Troy and the death of Agamemnon. 'I imagine the annunciation that founded Greece as made to Leda', he wrote in *A Vision*.

LEDA AND THE SWAN

A sudden blow: the great wings beating still
Above the staggering girl, her thighs caressed
By the dark webs, her nape caught in his bill,
He holds her helpless breast upon his breast.

How can those terrified vague fingers push
The feathered glory from her loosening thighs?

And how can body, laid in that white rush,
But feel the strange heart beating where it lies?

A shudder in the loins engenders there
The broken wall, the burning roof and tower
And Agamemnon dead.
      Being so caught up,
So mastered by the brute blood of the air,
Did she put on his knowledge with his power
Before the indifferent beak could let her drop?

In Yeats's scheme the 2,000 years of Greek civilisation were followed by the 2,000-year era of Christian civilisation, ushered in by the birth of Christ. In *A Vision* he describes the Christian era as 'feminine' and 'humane' with 'peace its main aim'. What will come next? In 'The Second Coming', prompted partly by the Russian Revolution, he foresees something terrible, an era described in *A Vision* as 'masculine' and 'harsh'. *Spiritus Mundi* in line 12 means 'world spirit' and signified for Yeats 'a universal memory and a "muse" of sorts that provides inspiration to the poet or writer'.

THE SECOND COMING

Turning and turning in the widening gyre
The falcon cannot see the falconer;
Things fall apart; the centre cannot hold;
Mere anarchy is loosed upon the world,
The blood-dimmed tide is loosed, and everywhere
The ceremony of innocence is drowned;
The best lack all conviction, while the worst
Are full of passionate intensity.

Surely some revolution is at hand;
Surely the Second Coming is at hand.
The Second Coming! Hardly are those words out
When a vast image out of *Spiritus Mundi*

Troubles my sight: somewhere in sands of the desert
A shape with lion body and the head of a man,
A gaze blank and pitiless as the sun,
Is moving its slow thighs, while all about it
Reel shadows of the indignant desert birds.
The darkness drops again; but now I know
That twenty centuries of stony sleep
Were vexed to nightmare by a rocking cradle,
And what rough beast, its hour come round at last,
Slouches towards Bethlehem to be born?

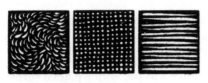

74

T.S. ELIOT
(1888–1965)

'La Figlia Che Piange' is undoubtedly a great poem and T.S. Eliot a great poet. It is, however, typical of much of Eliot's poetry in that it is incoherent. Why? The only certain answer is that Eliot chose it to be so. Critics have tied themselves in knots trying to give it coherence, but its greatness does not depend on their efforts. Rather it depends, like much of Eliot's poetry, on his genius for evocative phrases that give immediate pleasure – 'Weave, weave the sunlight in your hair', for example, or 'Simple and faithless as a smile and shake of the hand', or 'Her hair over her arms and her arms full of flowers'.

But why, it may be asked, has Eliot made his poem incoherent? It should be remembered that he was an educational elitist. Though expensively educated himself he opposed universal education, prophesying that 'our headlong rush to educate everybody' would lead to 'a deluge of barbarism'. Many intellectuals at the time shared these fears and wrote, as Eliot does here, in a deliberately incomprehensible manner to deter what they called 'the semi-educated'. The Italian title (meaning 'The girl who weeps') adds to the deliberate mystification. So does the unhelpful Latin quotation from Virgil's *Aeneid* 1.327, '*O quam te memorem virgo . . .*', that Eliot uses as his poem's epigraph. The Latin translates 'O maiden, how may I name thee?' and in the *Aeneid* these words are spoken by the hero Aeneas, addressing an unknown woman who is actually his mother, the goddess Venus, in disguise. None of this has any relevance to Eliot's poem beyond keeping the 'semi-educated' at bay.

LA FIGLIA CHE PIANGE
O QUAM TE MEMOREM VIRGO

Stand on the highest pavement of the stair –
Lean on a garden urn –
Weave, weave the sunlight in your hair –
Clasp your flowers to you with a pained surprise –
Fling them to the ground and turn
With a fugitive resentment in your eyes;
But weave, weave the sunlight in your hair.

So I would have had him leave,
So I would have had her stand and grieve,
So he would have left
As the soul leaves the body torn and bruised,
As the mind deserts the body it has used.
I should find
Some way incomparably light and deft,
Some way we both should understand,
Simple and faithless as a smile and shake of the hand.

She turned away, but with the autumn weather
Compelled my imagination many days,
Many days and many hours:
Her hair over her arms and her arms full of flowers.
And I wonder how they should have been together!
I should have lost a gesture and a pose.
Sometimes these cogitations still amaze
The troubled midnight and the noon's repose.

75

EZRA POUND
(1885–1972)

Li Po (AD 701–762) was one of the great poets of the Tang dynasty, reckoned the golden age of Chinese poetry. Ezra Pound did not know Chinese or Japanese, but he worked from a Japanese translation of Li Po's poem among the papers of Ernest Fenollosa, the American historian of Japanese art.

Li Po's poems characteristically record, as here in Pound's loose translation, the hardships and emotions of common people.

THE RIVER MERCHANT'S WIFE: A LETTER
AFTER LI PO

While my hair was still cut straight across my forehead
I played about the front gate, pulling flowers.
You came by on bamboo stilts, playing horse,
You walked about my seat, playing with blue plums,
And we went on living in the village of Chokan:
Two small people, without dislike or suspicion.

At fourteen I married My Lord you.
I never laughed, being bashful.
Lowering my head, I looked at the wall.
Called to, a thousand times, I never looked back.

At fifteen I stopped scowling,
I desired my dust to be mingled with yours
Forever and forever and forever.
Why should I climb the look out?

At sixteen you departed,
You went into far Ku-to-yen, by the river of swirling eddies,
And you have been gone five months.
The monkeys make sorrowful noise overhead.
You dragged your feet when you went out.
By the gate now, the moss is grown, the different mosses,
Too deep to clear them away!
The leaves fall early this autumn, in wind.
The paired butterflies are already yellow with August
Over the grass in the West garden;
They hurt me. I grow older.
If you are coming down through the narrows of the river Kiang,
Please let me know beforehand,
And I will come out to meet you
          As far as Cho-fu-Sa.

76

T.E. HULME
(1883–1917)

Thomas Ernest Hulme seems to have been the inventor of 'Imagism', which aimed at the exclusion of superfluous words and a concentration on 'the thing', whether subjective or objective. He was killed early in the First World War and left only a small number of poems, among them these three.

AUTUMN

A touch of cold in the Autumn night –
I walked abroad,
And saw the ruddy moon lean over a hedge
Like a red-faced farmer.
I did not stop to speak, but nodded,
And round about were the wistful stars
With white faces like town children.

ABOVE THE DOCK

Above the quiet dock in midnight,
Tangled in the tall mast's corded height,
Hangs the moon. What seemed so far away
Is but a child's balloon, forgotten after play.

THE EMBANKMENT
(THE FANTASIA OF A FALLEN GENTLEMAN ON
A COLD, BITTER NIGHT)

Once, in finesse of fiddles found I ecstasy,
In the flash of gold heels on the hard pavement.
Now see I
That warmth's the very stuff of poesy.
Oh, God, make small
The old star-eaten blanket of the sky,
That I may fold it round me and in comfort lie.

77

WILLIAM CARLOS WILLIAMS
(1883–1963)

William Carlos Williams told a friend that he was thinking of using *terza rima* in 'The Yachts', in imitation of Dante, but abandoned rhyme because he was carried away by his own feelings.

American tycoons such as J.P. Morgan and the Vanderbilts competed for the America's Cup in races off Newport, Rhode Island. Williams saw one of these races in 1935. In correspondence with Ezra Pound he confirmed that the point of the poem was to draw attention to the huge disparities of wealth in American society, particularly glaring in the depression of the 1930s.

As in other poems by Williams, the title is part of the poem.

THE YACHTS

contend in a sea which the land partly encloses
shielding them from the too-heavy blows
of an ungoverned ocean which when it chooses

tortures the biggest hulls, the best man knows
to pit against its beatings, and sinks them pitilessly.
Mothlike in mists, scintillant in the minute

brilliance of cloudless days, with broad bellying sails
they glide to the wind tossing green water
from their sharp prows while over them the crew crawls

ant-like, solicitously grooming them, releasing,
making fast as they turn, lean far over and having
caught the wind again, side by side, head for the mark.

In a well-guarded arena of open water surrounded by
lesser and greater craft which, sycophant, lumbering
and flittering follow them, they appear youthful, rare

as the light of a happy eye, live with the grace
of all that in the mind is feckless, free and
naturally to be desired. Now the sea which holds them

is moody, lapping their glossy sides, as if feeling
for some slightest flaw but fails completely.
Today no race. Then the wind comes again. The yachts

move, jockeying for a start, the signal is set and they
are off. Now the waves strike at them but they are too
well made, they slip through, though they take in canvas.

Arms with hands grasping seek to clutch at the prows.
Bodies thrown recklessly in the way are cut aside.
It is a sea of faces about them in agony, in despair

Until the horror of the race dawns staggering the mind,
the whole sea become an entanglement of watery bodies
lost to the world bearing what they cannot hold. Broken,

beaten, desolate, reaching from the dead to be taken up
they cry out, failing, failing! their cries rising
in waves still as the skillful yachts pass over.

78

HELENE JOHNSON
(1905–95)

Helene Johnson was one of the Black women poets of the Harlem Renaissance, a cultural movement of the 1920s and 1930s. Her reference in 'Bottled' to 'the bayonets we had "over there"' makes it clear that the poem's speaker is an American war veteran. This adds irony to the poem. The speaker, envisioning the 'darky' as carrying a spear and naked in a 'jungle,' displays his own racial prejudice. The poem is a dramatic monologue, not spoken in the poet's voice.

BOTTLED

Upstairs, on the third floor
Of the 135th Street Library
In Harlem, I saw a little
Bottle of sand, brown sand,
Just like the kids make pies
Out of down at the beach.
But the label said: 'This
Sand was taken from the Sahara desert.'
Imagine that! The Sahara desert!
Some bozo's been all the way to Africa to get some sand.

And yesterday, on Seventh Avenue,
I saw a darky dressed fit to kill
In yellow gloves and swallow-tail coat

And swirling a cane. And everyone
Was laughing at him. Me too,
At first, till I saw his face
When he stopped to hear an
Organ grinder grind out some jazz.
Boy! You should a seen that darky's face!
It just shone. Gee, he was happy!
And he began to dance. No
Charleston or Black Bottom for *him*.
No sir. He danced just as dignified
And slow. No, not slow either,
Dignified and *proud!* You couldn't
Call it slow, not with all the
Steps he did. You would a died to see him.

The crowd kept yellin' but he didn't hear,
Just kept on dancin' and twirlin' that cane,
And yellin' out loud every once in a while.

I know the crowd thought he was coo-coo.
But say, I was where I could see his face,
And somehow, I could see him dancin' in a jungle,
A real honest-to-cripe jungle, and he wouldn't have on them
Trick clothes – those yaller shoes and yaller gloves
And swallow-tail coat. He wouldn't have on nothing.
And he wouldn't be carrying no cane.
He'd be carrying a spear with a sharp fine point
Like the bayonets we had 'over there':
And the end of it would be dipped in some kind of
Hoo-doo poison. And he'd be dancin', black and naked and gleaming.
And he'd have rings in his ears and on his nose,
And bracelets and necklaces of elephants' teeth.
Gee, I bet he'd be beautiful then, all right.
No one would laugh at him then, I bet.

Say! That boy that took that sand from the Sahara desert
And put it in a little bottle on a shelf in the library;
That's what they done to this shine, ain't it? Bottled him.

Those trick shoes, trick coat, trick cane, trick everything; all bottle;
But, *inside* –
Gee, that poor shine!

79

LANGSTON HUGHES
(1902–67)

Langston Hughes was the foremost male poet of the Harlem Renaissance. This poem, like much of his work, shows his affiliation with the Civil Rights movement.

SOUTHERN MAMMY SINGS

Miss Gardner's in her garden.
Miss Yardman's in her yard.
Miss Michaelmas is at de mass
And I am gettin' tired!
    Lawd!
I am gettin' tired!

The nations they is fightin'
And the nations they done fit.
Sometimes I think that white folks
Ain't worth a little bit.
    No, m'am!
Ain't worth a little bit.

Last week they lynched a colored boy.
They hung him to a tree.
That colored boy ain't said a thing
But we all should be free.

Yes, m'am!
We all should be free.

Not meanin' to be sassy
And not meanin' to be smart –
But sometimes I think that white folks
Just ain't got no heart.
No, m'am!
Just ain't got no heart.

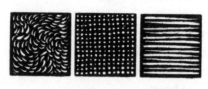

80

ELIZABETH BISHOP
(1911–79)

Elizabeth Bishop was born in Worcester, Massachusetts, but her father died before she was a year old and she and her mother went to live with her mother's parents in a coastal village in Nova Scotia. Her mother, who suffered from mental illness, was institutionalised when Bishop was five. Bishop continued to live with her grandparents until 1917 when her father's family claimed custody and took her back to Massachusetts, where she was unhappy and developed chronic asthma. Bishop's memories of Nova Scotia were idyllic and this poem, 'First Death in Nova Scotia', is set in the brief period when she lived there with her mother. Her cousin, whose real name was Frank, not Arthur, died when Bishop was four. The poem has been praised for its evocation of the staunchly loyal atmosphere of early twentieth-century Nova Scotia.

'Chromographs' are coloured lithographs; a 'loon' is a water bird; 'The Maple Leaf for Ever' was the unofficial Canadian national anthem.

FIRST DEATH IN NOVA SCOTIA

In the cold, cold parlor
my mother laid out Arthur
beneath the chromographs:
Edward, Prince of Wales,
with Princess Alexandra,
and King George with Queen Mary.
Below them on the table

stood a stuffed loon
shot and stuffed by Uncle
Arthur, Arthur's father.

Since Uncle Arthur fired
a bullet into him,
he hadn't said a word.
He kept his own counsel
on his white, frozen lake,
the marble-topped table.
His breast was deep and white,
cold and caressable;
his eyes were red glass,
much to be desired.

'Come,' said my mother,
'Come and say good-bye
to your little cousin Arthur.'
I was lifted up and given
one lily of the valley
to put in Arthur's hand.
Arthur's coffin was
a little frosted cake,
and the red-eyed loon eyed it
from his white, frozen lake.

Arthur was very small.
He was all white, like a doll
that hadn't been painted yet.
Jack Frost had started to paint him
the way he always painted
the Maple Leaf (Forever).
He had just begun on his hair,
a few red strokes, and then
Jack Frost had dropped the brush
and left him white, forever.

The gracious royal couples
were warm in red and ermine;
their feet were well wrapped up
in the ladies' ermine trains.
They invited Arthur to be
the smallest page at court.
But how could Arthur go,
clutching his tiny lily,
with his eyes shut up so tight
and the roads deep in snow?

81

W.H. AUDEN
(1907–73)

W.H. Auden's poem 'Musée des Beaux Arts' is based on an oil painting by Pieter Bruegel the Elder, entitled *Landscape with the Fall of Icarus*, in the Royal Museums of the Fine Arts of Belgium. In the foreground a ploughman is ploughing, a shepherd is tending his sheep and a man is sitting on the shore fishing. In the background is a bay and a ship with billowing sails. Icarus, the subject of the painting, is easily missed. His legs can be seen disappearing into the water just below the ship. The ploughman, shepherd and angler show no sign of having noticed that anything has happened, which is the point of Auden's poem.

In Greek mythology Icarus succeeds in flying with wings made by his father, Daedalus, using feathers secured by beeswax. But he flies too near the sun, the wax melts and he falls to his death.

MUSÉE DES BEAUX ARTS

About suffering they were never wrong,
The Old Masters: how well they understood
Its human position; how it takes place
While someone else is eating or opening a window or just
    walking dully along;
How, when the aged are reverently, passionately waiting
For the miraculous birth, there always must be
Children who did not specially want it to happen, skating
On a pond at the edge of the wood:

They never forgot
That even the dreadful martyrdom must run its course
Anyhow in a corner, some untidy spot
Where the dogs go on with their doggy life and the
        torturer's horse
Scratches its innocent behind on a tree.

In Brueghel's *Icarus*, for instance: how everything turns away
Quite leisurely from the disaster; the ploughman may
Have heard the splash, the forsaken cry,
But for him it was not an important failure; the sun shone
As it had to on the white legs disappearing into the green
Water; and the expensive delicate ship that must have seen
Something amazing, a boy falling out of the sky,
Had somewhere to get to and sailed calmly on.

82

LOUIS MACNEICE
(1907–63)

Louis MacNeice was Irish, born in Belfast, but educated at Marlborough College and Merton College, Oxford, where he got a first-class degree in classics in 1925. He took up a post as Lecturer in Classics at Birmingham University the same year. In his early life he had suffered several misfortunes. When he was six his mother was admitted to a nursing home suffering from depression and he did not see her again. She died in 1914. He had a brother who suffered from Down's syndrome and was sent to an institution in Scotland.

In 1930 MacNeice married Mary Ezra. She was Jewish and MacNeice's father, an Anglican minister, later a bishop, was horrified his son should marry a Jewish woman. He did not attend their registry office wedding, nor did Mary's parents, who opposed the marriage as they feared Down's syndrome might be hereditary. Mary gave birth to their son, Daniel, in 1934, but later the same year left MacNeice for a Russian-American graduate student who had been staying with the family.

This poem was written in 1944, as the war was drawing to a close, and its tone may reflect these misfortunes as well as the lessons the war had taught.

PRAYER BEFORE BIRTH

I am not yet born; O hear me.
Let not the bloodsucking bat or the rat or the stoat or the
    club-footed ghoul come near me.

I am not yet born, console me.
I fear that the human race may with tall walls wall me,
   with strong drugs dope me, with wise lies lure me,
      on black racks rack me, in blood-baths roll me.

I am not yet born; provide me
With water to dandle me, grass to grow for me, trees to talk
   to me, sky to sing to me, birds and a white light
      in the back of my mind to guide me.

I am not yet born; forgive me
for the sins that in me the world shall commit, my words
   when they speak to me, my thoughts when they think me,
      my treason engendered by traitors beyond me,
         my life when they murder by means of my
           hands, my death when they live me.

I am not yet born; rehearse me
In the parts I must play and the cues I must take when
   old men lecture me, bureaucrats hector me, mountains
      frown at me, lovers laugh at me, the white
         waves call me to folly and the desert calls
           me to doom, and the beggar refuses
           my gift and my children curse me.

I am not yet born; O hear me,
Let not the man who is beast or who thinks he is God
   come near me.

I am not yet born; O fill me
With strength against those who would freeze my
   humanity, would dragoon me into a lethal automaton,
      would make me a cog in a machine, a thing with
         one face, a thing, and against all those
           who would dissipate my entirety, would
           blow me like thistledown hither and

thither or hither and thither
like water held in the
hands would spill me.

Let them not make me a stone and let them not spill me.
Otherwise kill me.

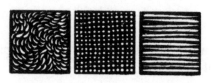

83

KEITH DOUGLAS
(1920–44)

Keith Douglas is chiefly known as a war poet. His memoir, *Alamein to Zem Zem*, records his experiences as a tank commander in North Africa. He was killed in Normandy shortly after the D-Day landings. But he wrote poems in Oxford before joining up, and 'Canoe' is one. Iffley is a village on the river east of Oxford.

CANOE

Well, I am thinking this may be my last
summer, but cannot lose even a part
of pleasure in the old-fashioned art
of idleness. I cannot stand aghast

at whatever doom hovers in the background;
while grass and buildings and the somnolent river,
who know they are allowed to last for ever,
exchange between them the whole subdued sound

of this hot time. What sudden fearful fate
can deter my shade wandering next year
from a return? Whistle and I will hear
and come again another evening, when this boat

travels with you alone toward Iffley:
as you lie looking up for thunder again,
this cool touch does not betoken rain;
it is my spirit that kisses your mouth lightly.

84

ALUN LEWIS
(1915–44)

Alun Lewis, a fine short-story writer as well as a poet, was commissioned in the South Wales Borderers and sent to Burma to join the campaign against the Japanese. On the morning of 5 March 1944 he was found shot in the head with his revolver in his hand. Suicide was suspected, but an army inquiry concluded it was an accident. 'Goodbye' was written for his wife, Gweno, in 1942.

GOODBYE

So we must say Goodbye, my darling,
And go, as lovers go, for ever;
Tonight remains, to pack and fix on labels
And make an end of lying down together.

I put a final shilling in the gas,
And watch you slip your dress below your knees
And lie so still I hear your rustling comb
Modulate the autumn in the trees.

And all the countless things I shall remember
Lay mummy-cloths of silence round my head;
I fill the carafe with a drink of water;
You say, 'We paid a guinea for this bed,'

And then, 'We'll leave some gas, a little warmth
For the next resident, and these dry flowers,'
And turn your face away, afraid to speak
The big word, that Eternity is ours.

Your kisses close my eyes and yet you stare
As though god struck a child with nameless fears;
Perhaps the water glitters and discloses
Time's chalice and its limpid useless tears.

Everything we renounce except our selves;
Selfishness is the last of all to go;
Our sighs are exhalations of the earth,
Our footprints leave a track across the snow.

We made the universe to be our home,
Our nostrils took the wind to be our breath,
Our hearts are massive towers of delight,
We stride across the seven seas of death.

Yet when all's done you'll keep the emerald
I placed upon your finger in the street;
And I will keep the patches that you sewed
On my old battledress tonight, my sweet.

85

HENRY REED
(1914–86)

Henry Reed was called up in 1941 and spent most of the war as a Japanese translator. This poem is one of his 'Lessons of the War' series, which mock the 'basic training' delivered to new recruits by NCOs.

JUDGING DISTANCES

Not only how far away, but the way that you say it
Is very important. Perhaps you may never get
The knack of judging a distance, but at least you know
How to report on a landscape: the central sector,
The right of arc and that, which we had last Tuesday,
    And at least you know

That maps are of time, not place, so far as the army
Happens to be concerned – the reason being,
Is one which need not delay us. Again, you know
There are three kinds of tree, three only, the fir and the poplar,
And those which have bushy tops to; and lastly
    That things only seem to be things.

A barn is not called a barn, to put it more plainly,
Or a field in the distance, where sheep may be safely grazing.
You must never be over-sure. You must say, when reporting:
At five o'clock in the central sector is a dozen

Of what appear to be animals; whatever you do,
  Don't call the bleeders *sheep*.

I am sure that's quite clear; and suppose, for the sake of example,
The one at the end, asleep, endeavours to tell us
What he sees over there to the west, and how far away,
After first having come to attention. There to the west,
On the fields of summer the sun and the shadows bestow
  Vestments of purple and gold.

The still white dwellings are like a mirage in the heat,
And under the swaying elms a man and a woman
Lie gently together. Which is, perhaps, only to say
That there is a row of houses to the left of arc,
And that under some poplars a pair of what appear to be humans
  Appear to be loving.

Well that, for an answer, is what we might rightly call
Moderately satisfactory only, the reason being,
Is that two things have been omitted, and those are important.
The human beings, now: in what direction are they,
And how far away, would you say? And do not forget
  There may be dead ground in between.

There may be dead ground in between; and I may not have got
The knack of judging a distance; I will only venture
A guess that perhaps between me and the apparent lovers
(Who, incidentally, appear by now to have finished)
At seven o'clock from the houses, is roughly a distance
  Of about one year and a half.

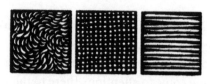

86

LOUIS SIMPSON
(1923–2012)

Louis Simpson served with the US 101st Airborne Division, and 'Carentan O Carentan' is based on his experience of a bloody engagement in the Cherbourg peninsula in June 1944.

CARENTAN O CARENTAN

Trees in the old days used to stand
And shape a shady lane
Where lovers wandered hand in hand
Who came from Carentan.

This was the shining green canal
Where we came two by two
Walking at combat-interval.
Such trees we never knew.

The day was early June, the ground
Was soft and bright with dew.
Far away the guns did sound,
But here the sky was blue.

The sky was blue, but there a smoke
Hung still above the sea

Where the ships together spoke
To towns we could not see.

Could you have seen us through a glass
You would have said a walk
Of farmers out to turn the grass,
Each with his own hay-fork.

The watchers in their leopard suits
Waited till it was time,
And aimed between the belt and boot
And let the barrel climb.

I must lie down at once, there is
A hammer at my knee.
And call it death or cowardice,
Don't count again on me.

Everything's all right, Mother,
Everyone gets the same
At one time or another.
It's all in the game.

I never strolled, nor ever shall,
Down such a leafy lane.
I never drank in a canal,
Nor ever shall again.

There is a whistling in the leaves
And it is not the wind,
The twigs are falling from the knives
That cut men to the ground.

Tell me, Master-Sergeant,
The way to turn and shoot.
But the Sergeant's silent
That taught me how to do it.

O Captain, show us quickly
Our place upon the map.
But the Captain's sickly
And taking a long nap.

Lieutenant, what's my duty,
My place in the platoon?
He too's a sleeping beauty,
Charmed by that strange tune.

Carentan O Carentan
Before we met with you
We never yet had lost a man
Or known what death could do.

RICHARD WILBUR
(1921–2017)

Richard Wilbur was the second poet laureate of the United States, and won many awards. 'The Death of a Toad' was first published in *Poetry* magazine in 1948.

THE DEATH OF A TOAD

A toad the power mower caught,
Chewed and clipped of a leg, with a hobbling hop has got
To the garden verge, and sanctuaried him
Under the cineraria leaves, in the shade
Of the ashen and heartshaped leaves, in a dim,
Low, and a final glade.

The rare original heartsblood goes,
Spends in the earthen hide, in the folds and wizenings, flows
In the gutters of the banked and staring eyes. He lies
As still as if he would return to stone,
And soundlessly attending, dies
Toward some deep monotone,

Toward misted and ebullient seas
And cooling shores, toward lost Amphibia's emperies.
Day dwindles, drowning, and at length is gone
In the wide and antique eyes, which still appear
To watch, across the castrate lawn,
The haggard daylight steer.

RANDALL JARRELL
(1914–65)

When the Second World War broke out Randall Jarrell was teaching at the University of Texas, Austin. In 1942, shortly after the Japanese attack on Pearl Harbor, he joined the United States Army Air Force as a navigation instructor, serving on airfields in Texas and Illinois, and on a base for Flying Fortresses in the Arizona desert. Though he did not have a combat role he listened to the flight crews returning from sorties, with their talk of suffering, fear and death. He realised that air warfare is unique, isolating the individual miles above the earth and his fellow men, and confronting him with merciless and devastatingly deadly technology. Using this knowledge, he wrote some of the best-known American war poems. Towards the end of his life he suffered from depression, possibly suffering from survivor guilt, and his death in a car accident may have been suicide.

This poem traces a soldier's drift into dream, which happens in stanza 4. As in many of Jarrell's poems the soldier becomes childlike, and the 'Causes' in stanza 7 seem like his parents bending over him.

ABSENT WITH OFFICIAL LEAVE

The lights are beginning to go out in the barracks.
They persist or return, as the wakeful hollow,
But only for an instant; then the windows blacken
For all the hours of the soldier's life.

It is life into which he composes his body.
He covers his ears with his pillow, and begins to drift
(Like the plumes the barracks trail into the sky)
Past the laughs, the quarrels, and the breath of others

To the ignorant countries where civilians die
Inefficiently, in their spare time, for nothing. . . .
The curved roads hopping through the aimless green
Dismay him, and the cottages where people cry

For themselves and, sometimes, for the absent soldier –
Who inches through hedges where the hunters sprawl
For birds, for birds; who turns in ecstasy
Before the slow small fires the women light,

His charmed limbs, all endearing from the tub.
He dozes, and the washed locks trail like flax
Down the dark face; and the unaccusing eyes
That even the dream's eyes are averted from

See the wind puff down the chimney, warm the hands
White with the blossoms it pretends are snow. . . .
He moans like a bear in his enchanted sleep,
And the grave mysterious beings of his years –

The Causes that mourn above his agony like trees –
Are moved for their child, and bend across his limbs
The one face opening for his life, the eyes
That look without shame even into his.

And the child awakes, and sees around his life
The night that is never silent – broken with the sighs
And patient breathing of the dark companions
With whom he labors, sleeps, and dies.

JOHN PUDNEY
(1909–77)

During the Second World War John Pudney was commissioned into the Royal Air Force as an intelligence officer and as a member of the Air Ministry's Creative Writers Unit. 'For Johnny' became one of the war's most popular poems in England and featured in the 1945 British war film *The Way to the Stars*, which was distributed in the United States as *Johnny in the Clouds*.

FOR JOHNNY

Do not despair
For Johnny-head-in-air,
He sleeps as sound
As Johnny underground.

Fetch out no shroud
For Johnny-in-the-cloud,
And keep your tears
For him in after years.

Better by far
For Johnny-the-bright-star;
To keep your head,
And see his children fed.

LOIS CLARK

Nothing seems to be known about Lois Clark, not even the dates of her birth and death, apart from this poem, 'Picture from the Blitz', from which it can be deduced that she drove a stretcher-party car during the London Blitz, which meant she was often among the first to arrive at the site of a bombing.

'Flack' in stanza 3, usually spelt 'flak', means spent ammunition from anti-aircraft guns, which in German are *Fliegerabwehrkanone*. The English word is an acronym of this.

PICTURE FROM THE BLITZ

After all these years
I can still close my eyes and see
her sitting there,
in her big armchair,
grotesque under an open sky,
framed by the jagged lines of her broken house.

Sitting there,
a plump homely person,
steel needles still in her work-rough hands;
grey with dust, stiff with shock,
but breathing,
no blood or distorted limbs;

breathing but stiff with shock,
knitting unravelling on her apron'd knee.

They have taken the stretchers off my car
and I am running
under the pattering flack
over a mangled garden;
treading on something soft
and fighting the rising nausea –
only a far-flung cushion, bleeding feathers.

They lift her gently
out of her great armchair,
tenderly,
under the open sky,
a shock-frozen woman trailing khaki wool.

91

THEODORE ROETHKE
(1908–63)

Theodore Roethke's father was a market gardener with 25 acres of greenhouses in Saginaw, Michigan, and the greenhouse became for Roethke 'my symbol for the whole of life, a womb, a heaven-on-earth' – words now inscribed on his memorial at Saginaw.

'Smilax' are climbing, flowering plants; 'dirt' is American for soil; a 'whiffet' can mean an insignificant person or a little dog.

FRAU BAUMAN, FRAU SCHMIDT AND FRAU SCHWARTZE

Gone the three ancient ladies
Who creaked on the greenhouse ladders,
Reaching up white strings
To wind, to wind
The sweet-pea tendrils, the smilax,
Nasturtiums, the climbing
Roses, to straighten
Carnations, red
Chrysanthemums; the stiff
Stems, jointed like corn,
They tied and tucked, –
These nurses of nobody else.
Quicker than birds, they dipped
Up and sifted the dirt;

They sprinkled and shook;
They stood astride pipes,
Their skirts billowing out wide into tents,
Their hands twinkling with wet;
Like witches they flew along rows
Keeping creation at ease;
With a tendril for needle
They sewed up the air with a stem;
They teased out the seed that the cold kept asleep, –
All the coils, loops, and whorls.
They trellised the sun; they plotted for more than themselves.

I remember how they picked me up, a spindly kid,
Pinching and poking my thin ribs
Till I lay in their laps, laughing,
Weak as a whiffet;
Now, when I'm alone and cold in my bed,
They still hover over me,
These ancient leathery crones,
With their bandannas stiffened with sweat,
And their thorn-bitten wrists,
And their snuff-laden breath blowing lightly over me in
    my first sleep.

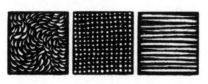

92

PHILIP LARKIN
(1922–85)

Larkin described 'The Explosion' as 'a poem that isn't especially like me, or like what I fancy I'm supposed to be like'. He said that he had heard a ballad called 'The Trimdon Grange Explosion', by the concert-hall performer Thomas Armstrong, on a record, *The Collier's Rant: Mining Songs of the Northumberland-Durham Coalfield*. 'I thought it very moving and it produced the poem. It made me want to write the same thing, a mine disaster with a vision of immortality at the end – that's the point of the eggs.' The disaster happened at Trimdon near Durham on 15 February 1882. Seventy-four men and boys died.

THE EXPLOSION

On the day of the explosion
Shadows pointed towards the pithead:
In the sun the slagheap slept.

Down the lane came men in pitboots
Coughing oath-edged talk and pipe-smoke,
Shouldering off the freshened silence.

One chased after rabbits; lost them;
Came back with a nest of lark's eggs;
Showed them; lodged them in the grasses.

So they passed in beards and moleskins,
Fathers, brothers, nicknames, laughter,
Through the tall gates standing open.

At noon, there came a tremor; cows
Stopped chewing for a second; sun,
Scarfed as in a heat-haze, dimmed.

The dead go on before us, they
Are sitting in God's house in comfort,
We shall see them face to face –

Plain as lettering in the chapels
It was said, and for a second
Wives saw men of the explosion

Larger than in life they managed –
Gold as on a coin, or walking
Somehow from the sun towards them,

One showing the eggs unbroken.

D.J. ENRIGHT
(1920–2002)

D.J. Enright was the finest of the Movement poets, with the possible exception of Larkin, and the subject of this poem would have been far outside Larkin's range.

ON THE DEATH OF A CHILD

The greatest griefs shall find themselves
    inside the smallest cage.
It's only then that we can hope to tame
    their rage,

The monsters we must live with. For
    it will not do
To hiss humanity because one human threw
Us out of heart and home. Or part

At odds with life because one baby failed
    to live.
Indeed, as little as its subject, is
    the wreath we give –

The big words fail to fit. Like giant boxes
Round small bodies. Taking up improper room,
Where so much withering is, and so much bloom.

THOM GUNN
(1913–2004)

In 1954, soon after the publication of his first collection, *Fighting Terms*, the English poet Thom Gunn moved to California with his partner, Mike Kitay, and lived the rest of his life in San Francisco, becoming a prominent figure in the gay counter-culture. He lost many friends in the 1980s AIDS epidemic, writing elegies for them in *The Man with Night Sweats* (1992), in which this poem first appeared.

THE HUG

It was your birthday, we had drunk and dined
    Half of the night with our old friend
      Who'd showed us in the end
    To a bed I reached in one drunk stride.
      Already I lay snug,
And drowsy with the wine dozed on one side.

I dozed, I slept. My sleep broke on a hug,
      Suddenly, from behind,
In which the full lengths of our bodies pressed:
      Your instep to my heel,
    My shoulder-blades against your chest.
    It was not sex, but I could feel
    The whole strength of your body set,
      Or braced, to mine,

And locking me to you
As if we were still twenty-two
When our grand passion had not yet
Become familial.
My quick sleep had deleted all
Of intervening time and place.
I only knew
The stay of your secure firm dry embrace.

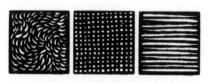

95

TED HUGHES
(1930–98)

Hughes started writing *Crow: From the Life and Songs of the Crow* in 1966, three years after his wife Sylvia Plath's suicide. Some of the poems in it seem pointlessly violent and destructive. This one does not.

THE BLACK BEAST

Where is the Black Beast?
Crow, like an owl, swivelled his head.
Where is the Black Beast?
Crow hid in its bed, to ambush it.
Where is the Black Beast?
Crow sat in its chair, telling loud lies against the Black Beast.
Where is it?
Crow shouted after midnight, pounding the wall with a last.
Where is the Black Beast?
Crow split his enemy's skull to the pineal gland.
Where is the Black Beast?
Crow crucified a frog under a microscope, he peered into
    the brain of a dogfish.
Where is the Black Beast?
Crow killed his brother and turned him inside out to stare
    at his colour.
Where is the Black Beast?
Crow roasted the earth to a clinker, he charged into space –

Where is the Black Beast?
The silences of space decamped, space flitted in every direction –
Where is the Black Beast?
Crow flailed immensely through the vacuum, he screeched
    after the disappearing stars –
Where is it? Where is the Black Beast?

96

SYLVIA PLATH
(1932–63)

This poem was written in the burst of creativity Sylvia Plath experienced in the months before her death. She gave birth to her son, Nicholas, in January 1962. In July she discovered her husband was having an affair with Assia Wevill, and they separated in September. In December Plath returned to London from Devon and rented a flat at 23 Fitzroy Road, where Yeats had once lived. The winter of 1962–3 was one of the coldest for a century. The pipes froze, Nicholas and his elder sister, Frieda, were often ill. There was no phone. On the morning of 11 February 1963 Plath was found dead, with her head in the gas oven. She had sealed the door between her and the sleeping children (Frieda aged two and Nicholas, one) with tape, towels and cloths.

NICK AND THE CANDLESTICK

I am a miner. The light burns blue.
Waxy stalacmites
Drip and thicken, tears

The earthen womb
Exudes from its dead boredom.
Black bat airs

Wrap me, raggy shawls,
Cold homicides.
They weld to me like plums.

Old cave of calcium
Icicles, old echoer.
Even the newts are white,

Those holy Joes.
And the fish, the fish –
Christ! they are panes of ice,

A vice of knives,
A piranha
Religion, drinking

Its first communion out of my live toes.
The candle
Gulps and recovers its small altitude,

Its yellows hearten.
O love, how did you get here?
O embryo

Remembering, even in sleep,
Your crossed position.
The blood blooms clean

In you, ruby.
The pain
You wake to is not yours.

Love, love,
I have hung our cave with roses,
With soft rugs –

The last of Victoriana.
Let the stars
Plummet to their dark address,

Let the mercuric
Atoms that cripple drip
Into the terrible well,

You are the one
Solid the spaces lean on, envious.
You are the baby in the barn.

97

R.S. THOMAS
(1913–2000)

R.S. Thomas became notorious as a Welsh nationalist who resented the Anglicisation of the Welsh nation, and supported the fire-bombing of English holiday cottages in rural Wales. As a clergyman, he has been ridiculed for condemning modern amenities, such as refrigerators and washing machines, while addressing an impoverished rural congregation who longed for such labour-saving devices. What he will be remembered for, however, is his poetry. His religious life was often dark. Like Gerard Manley Hopkins, he was sometimes tormented by a sense of God's absence. 'The Bright Field', one of his best-loved poems, places the spiritual life above everything else.

> I have seen the sun break through
> to illuminate a small field
> for a while, and gone my way
> and forgotten it. But that was the pearl
> of great price, the one field that had
> the treasure in it. I realize now,
> that I must give all that I have
> to possess it. Life is not hurrying
>
> on to a receding future, nor hankering after
> an imagined past. It is the turning
> aside like Moses to the miracle

of the lit bush, to a brightness
that seemed as transitory as your youth
once, but is the eternity that awaits you.

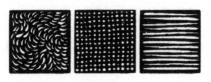

98

SEAMUS HEANEY
(1939–2013)

When Seamus Heaney was 12 he won a scholarship to St Columb's College, a Roman Catholic boarding school in Derry. His brother Christopher was killed in a car accident while he was there.

'Mid-Term Break' was one of his earliest poems, first printed in *Eleven Poems* (1965), and reprinted in *Death of a Naturalist* (1966).

MID-TERM BREAK

I sat all morning in the college sick bay,
Counting bells knolling classes to a close.
At two o'clock our neighbours drove me home.

In the porch I met my father crying –
He had always taken funerals in his stride –
And Big Jim Evans saying it was a hard blow.

The baby cooed and laughed and rocked the pram
When I came in, and I was embarrassed
By old men standing up to shake my hand

And tell me they were 'sorry for my trouble'.
Whispers informed strangers I was the eldest,
Away at school, as my mother held my hand

In hers and coughed out angry tearless sighs.
At ten o'clock the ambulance arrived
With the corpse, stanched and bandaged by the nurses.

Next morning I went up into the room. Snowdrops
And candles soothed the bedside; I saw him
For the first time in six weeks. Paler now,

Wearing a poppy bruise on his left temple,
He lay in the four foot box as in his cot.
No gaudy scars, the bumper knocked him clear.

A four foot box, a foot for every year.

99

MAYA ANGELOU
(1928–2014)

I Know Why the Caged Bird Sings was the title of Maya Angelou's 1969 autobiography. It was taken from 'Sympathy', a poem by the African-American poet Paul Laurence Dunbar. The third stanza of this poem reads:

> I know why the caged bird sings, ah me,
>> When his wing is bruised and his bosom sore, –
> When he beats his bars and he would be free;
> It is not a carol of joy or glee,
>> But a prayer that he sends from his heart's deep core,
> But a plea, that upward to Heaven he flings –
> I know why the caged bird sings!

This was the origin, too, of Angelou's most famous poem, 'Caged Bird'.

CAGED BIRD

A free bird leaps
on the back of the wind
and floats downstream
till the current ends
and dips his wing
in the orange sun rays
and dares to claim the sky.

But a bird that stalks
down his narrow cage
can seldom see through
his bars of rage
his wings are clipped and
his feet are tied
so he opens his throat to sing.

The caged bird sings
with a fearful trill
of things unknown
but longed for still
and his tune is heard
on the distant hill
for the caged bird
sings of freedom.

The free bird thinks of another breeze
and the trade winds soft through the sighing trees
and the fat worms waiting on a dawn bright lawn
and he names the sky his own.

But a caged bird stands on the grave of dreams
his shadow shouts on a nightmare scream
his wings are clipped and his feet are tied
so he opens his throat to sing.

The caged bird sings
with a fearful trill
of things unknown
but longed for still
and his tune is heard
on the distant hill
for the caged bird
sings of freedom.

100

LES MURRAY
(1938–2019)

This poem is from the Australian poet Les Murray's 2015 collection, *Waiting for the Past*.

VERTIGO

Last time I fell in a shower room
I bled like a tumbril dandy
and the hotel longed to be rid of me.
Taken to the town clinic, I
described how I tripped on a steel rim
and found my head in the wardrobe.
Scalp-sewn and knotted and flagged
I thanked the Frau Doktor and fled,
wishing the grab-bar of age might
be bolted to all civilization
and thinking of Rome's eighth hill
heaped up out of broken amphorae.

When, anytime after sixty,
or anytime before, you stumble,
over two stairs and club your forehead
on rake or hoe, bricks or fuel-drums,
that's the time to call the purveyor
of steel pipe and indoor railings,

and soon you'll be grasping up landings,
having left your balance in the car
from which please God you'll never
see the launchway of tires off a brink.
Later comes the sunny day when
street detail whitens blindly to mauve

and people hurry you, or wait, quiet.

ACKNOWLEDGEMENTS

I should like to thank my editor, Julian Loose. I have benefited from his expert guidance for many years, and the anthology was his idea. Rachael Lonsdale and Lucy Buchan of Yale University Press have been wonderfully helpful and patient in preparing the text for the printer, and, as always, my wife Gill has been my mainstay and wisest critic.

We are grateful to the following for permission to reproduce copyright material:
An extract from Homer: *The Odyssey*, translated by Emily Wilson, copyright © 2018 by Emily Wilson. Used by permission of W.W. Norton & Company, Inc.; the poem from *Sappho: A New Translation*, translated by Mary Barnard, copyright © 1958 by The Regents of the University of California. Renewed 1986 by Mary Barnard. Published by the University of California Press; an extract from *Tales from Ovid: Twenty-four Passages from the Metamorphoses* by Ted Hughes, Faber & Faber Ltd, 1997. Reproduced by permission of the publisher; the poem 'Wie langsam kriechet sie dahin' by Heinrich Heine, translated by Louis Untermeyer, from *Paradox and Poet*, Harcourt Brace, 1937. Reproduced by special permission of Laurence S. Untermeyer for the Estate; the poem 'Der Panther (Im Jardin des Plantes, Paris)' by Rainer Maria Rilke, from *Possibility of Being*, translated by J.B. Leishman, copyright © 1955, 1977 by New Directions Publishing Corp. Translation © The Hogarth Press, Ltd, 1960, 1964. Reproduced by permission of New Directions Publishing Corp.; the poem 'In my craft or sullen art' by Dylan Thomas, from *The Collected Poems of Dylan Thomas: The Centenary Edition*, Weidenfeld and

Nicolson, 2014, copyright © The Dylan Thomas Trust / *The Poems of Dylan Thomas*, copyright © 1946 by New Directions Publishing Corp. Reproduced with permission of David Higham Associates; and New Directions Publishing Corp.; the poem 'Out, Out' by Robert Frost, from *The Collected Poems of Robert Frost*, 2016, edited by Edward Connery Lathem, copyright © 1916, 1969 by Henry Holt and Company, copyright © 1944 by Robert Frost. Reproduced with permission of The Random House Group Limited, and Henry Holt and Company. All rights reserved; the poem 'The Cool Web' by Robert Graves from *Collected Poems*, 2/e, Cassell, 1959, p. 56. Reproduced with permission of Carcanet Press, Manchester, UK; the poem 'Snake' by D.H. Lawrence, from *The Cambridge Edition of the Works of DH Lawrence: The Poems*, Cambridge University Press, copyright © 2013 by Cambridge University Press. Reproduced by permission of Paper Lion Ltd, The Estate of Frieda Lawrence Ravagli and Cambridge University Press; the poem 'Rouen April 26 – May 24 1915' by May Wedderburn Cannan, originally published in *In War Time*, Blackwell, 1917. Reproduced with kind permission of Mrs Clara May Abrahams; the poem 'La Figlia che Piange' by T.S. Eliot, from *The Complete Poems and Plays*, Faber & Faber Ltd, 2004, copyright © 1969 by Valerie Eliot. Reproduced by permission of the publisher; the poem 'The River Merchant's Wife': A Letter by Ezra Pound, original by Rihaku, from *Personae*, Faber & Faber Ltd, copyright © 1926 by Ezra Pound. Reproduced by permission of the publisher; and New Directions Publishing Corp.; the poem 'The Yachts' by William Carlos Williams from *The Complete Collected Poems of William Carlos Williams 1906-1938* / *The Collected Poems: Volume I, 1909-1939,* New Directions Publishing Corp., copyright © 1938 by New Directions Publishing Corp. Reproduced with permission of Carcanet Press, Manchester, UK; and New Directions Publishing Corp.; the poem 'Bottled' by Helene Johnson, from *This Waiting for Love: Helene Johnson, Poet of the Harlem Renaissance*, edited by Verner D. Mitchell, copyright © 2000 by the University of Massachusetts Press; the poem 'Southern Mammy Sings' by Langston Hughes from *The Collected Works of Langston Hughes: The poems 1941-1950, Vol 2*, ed. Woodrow Wilson, University of Missouri Press, 2001 / *The Collected Poems of Langston Hughes*, ed. Arnold Rampersad with David Roessel, copyright © 1994 by the Estate of Langston Hughes. Reproduced by permission of David

Higham Associates, and Alfred A. Knopf, an imprint of the Knopf Doubleday Publishing Group, a division of Penguin Random House LLC. All rights reserved; the poem 'First Death in Nova Scotia' by Elizabeth Bishop from *The Complete Poems 1927–1979*, published by Chatto and Windus, copyright © 1979, 1983, 2011 by Alice Helen Methfessel / *Poems* by Elizabeth Bishop, copyright © 2011 by The Alice H. Methfessel Trust. Publisher's Note and compilation copyright © 2011 by Farrar, Straus and Giroux. Reproduced by permission of The Random House Group Limited and Farrar, Straus and Giroux; the poem 'Musée des Beaux Arts' by W.H. Auden, from *Collected Poems* by W.H. Auden, edited by Edward Mendelson, copyright © 1940 and © renewed 1968 by W.H. Auden. Reproduced by permission of Random House, an imprint and division of Penguin Random House LLC; and the Estate on behalf of Curtis Brown Limited, NY. All rights reserved; the poem 'Prayer before birth' by Louis MacNeice from *The Collected Poems of Louis MacNeice*, edited by Peter Donald, Faber & Faber Ltd, 2016. Reproduced by permission of David Higham Associates; the poem 'Judging Distances' from 'Lessons of War' by Henry Reed from *Collected Poems*, edited and introduced by Jon Stallworthy, Oxford University Press, 1991. Reproduced with permission of the Licensor through PLSClear; the poem 'Carentan O Carentan' by Louis Simpson from *The Owner of the House: New Collected Poems 1940–2001*, copyright © 2001 by Louis Simpson. Reproduced with permission of The Permissions Company, LLC on behalf of BOA Editions, Ltd, www.boaeditions.org; the poem 'The Death of a Toad' by Richard Wilbur from *Ceremony and Other Poems* by Richard Wilbur, copyright © 1950, renewed 1978 by Richard Wilbur. Reproduced by permission of Houghton Mifflin Harcourt Publishing Company. All rights reserved; the poem 'Absent with Official Leave' by Randall Jarrell from *The Complete Poems*, Faber & Faber Ltd, 1971, copyright © 1996, renewed 1997 by Mary von S. Jarrell. Reproduced by permission of Faber & Faber Ltd; and Farrar, Straus and Giroux; the poem 'For Johnny' by John S. Pudney from *Dispersal Point and Other Air Poems*, Bodley Head, 1942. Reproduced by permission of David Higham Associates; the poem 'Frau Bauman, Frau Schmidt and Frau Schwartze' by Theodore Roethke, from *Collected Poems* by Theodore Roethke, Faber & Faber Ltd, copyright © 1952 by Theodore Roethke, copyright © 1966 and renewed 1994 by

Beatrice Lushington. Reproduced by permission of the publisher; and Doubleday, an imprint of the Knopf Doubleday Publishing Group, a division of Penguin Random House LLC. All rights reserved; the poem 'The Explosion' by Philip Larkin, from *The Complete Poems of Philip Larkin*, edited by Archie Burnett, Faber & Faber Ltd, 2014, copyright © 2012 by The Estate of Philip Larkin. Reproduced by permission of the publisher; and Farrar, Straus and Giroux; the poem 'On the Death of a Child' by D.J. Enright, from *Selected Poems*, Oxford University Press, 1990. Reproduced by permission of Watson, Little Ltd; the poem 'The Hug' by Thom Gunn, from *The Man with Night Sweats*, Faber & Faber Ltd, 1992 / *Collected Poems* by Thom Gunn, copyright © 1994 by Thom Gunn. Reproduced by permission of the publisher; and Farrar, Straus and Giroux; the poem 'The Black Beast' by Ted Hughes, from *Crow*, Faber & Faber Ltd, 2001. Reproduced by permission of the publisher; the poem 'Nick and the Candlestick' by Sylvia Plath from *Ariel* / *The Collected Poems*, Faber & Faber Ltd, copyright © 1960, 1965, 1971, 1981 by the Estate of Sylvia Plath. Editorial material copyright © 1981 by Ted Hughes. Used by permission of the publisher and HarperCollins Publishers; the poem 'The Bright Field' by R.S. Thomas, from *Collected Poems 1945–1990*, Orion, copyright © R.S. Thomas 1993. Reproduced by permission of The Orion Publishing Group, London; the poem 'Mid-Term Break' by Seamus Heaney, from *Death of a Naturalist*, Faber & Faber Ltd, 1966 / *Opened Ground: Selected Poems 1966–1996* by Seamus Heaney, copyright © 1998 by Seamus Heaney. Reproduced by permission of the publisher; and Farrar, Straus and Giroux; the poem 'Caged Bird' by Maya Angelou from *Shaker, Why Don't You Sing?* by Maya Angelou, copyright © 1983 by Maya Angelou. Reproduced by permission of Little, Brown Book Group; and Random House, an imprint and division of Penguin Random House LLC. All rights reserved; and the poem 'Vertigo' by Les Murray, from *Waiting for the Past*, Carcanet, 2015, copyright © 2015 by Les Murray. Reproduced with permission of Carcanet Press, Manchester, UK; and Farrar, Straus and Giroux.

In some instances we have been unable to trace the owners of copyright material, and we would appreciate any information that would enable us to do so.